The Moment that *Changes Everything*

BREAK THR⬦UGH

When to **Give In,**
How to **Push Back**

TIM CLINTON
PAT SPRINGLE

WORTHY
PUBLISHING

> **From Tim:**
> *To Julie and our children, Megan and Zach—you make*
> *loving fun. I can't imagine a day without you.*
>
> **From Pat:**
> *For Joyce, who has taught me more about the meaning*
> *and power of love than anyone on the planet.*

CONTENTS

Acknowledgments

This book would not have been possible without the support, input, and encouragement of our family, friends, and colleagues.

We want to thank:

"Team AACC"—including Laura Faidley, Ryan Carboneau, Hitomi Makino, and Leonard Davidson—who gave invaluable assistance in crafting and editing the manuscript.

Kris Bearss, executive editor at Worthy Publishing, who believed in the message of this book.

Our professors, mentors, pastors—and many from ages past—whose piercing insights about relationships form the core of our message.

The dozens of courageous men and women whose stories are found (if sometimes disguised) in these pages. They have wrestled with deep hurts, disappointments, and distorted perceptions, but they never gave up. They are examples for all of us.

And most of all, our Lord and Savior Jesus Christ, who daily blesses us with his love, grace, and forgiveness. "The steadfast love of the LORD never ceases; his mercies never come to an end; they are new every morning; great is your faithfulness" (Lamentations 3:22–23 ESV).

A NEW DAY FOR YOUR RELATIONSHIPS

Let's be honest. None of us had a perfect family. None of us have perfect friends or perfect coworkers, perfect children or perfect spouses. We all carry relational wounds. And many of us grew up experiencing highly imperfect relationships as the norm. So it's no wonder that we go through life with a skewed understanding of love, often repeating the very same patterns that we disliked as kids.

We may think we are loving our deadbeat dad, our alcoholic spouse, or our wayward child by continually rescuing them, but our actions are a far cry from true connection. In reality, we may be trying to "love" someone in an attempt to satisfy our "need" for them. And if that is so, it's a shallow substitute for the love God longs for us to experience.

So let's not even call it love.

By the time you're finished with this book, however, you'll not only recognize love for all that it is, but break through the fog of your relationships into the light of an amazing new day for you and for those you love the most.

CHAPTER 1

IN THE NAME OF LOVE

LIKE THUNDER NEEDS RAIN

LIKE THE PREACHER NEEDS PAIN . . .

I NEED YOUR LOVE

—"Hawkmoon 269" *by U2*

• Sarah and Matt have been dating for about five years. "We've had some really good moments," she sighs. "But right now, I'm just not feeling it. More than anything, I want to know that he loves me. I want to feel safe with him . . . to be happily married someday.

"Of course, we've been together long enough that I've seen some patterns I don't like. Matt gets upset easily. Sometimes, he'll yell and scream at me for no reason at all. And his work is so demanding that he sometimes completely tunes me out . . . for weeks at a time. He's also stayed close with some old girlfriends, but he promises me that it's not a big deal.

"These things used to bother me, but I've learned that's just how Matt is. Most people can't see it, but he really is a good person. My parents and close friends keep telling me to break up with him, but they just don't understand him. The truth is, I'd rather be with Matt than be alone. And, besides, he needs me."

• Janelle, a frustrated mom, tries to explain herself. "You just don't understand," she insists. "The reason I haven't told my husband about Tommy's drug use and gambling is because I love him so much. I know Tommy has blown a lot of money— my money, our money. But I worry that if my husband found out how bad it really is, he'd kick Tommy out of the house. That's why I've lied to him repeatedly about Tommy . . . How could I not? Tommy's my son.

"Tommy's biological father was killed when he was very young, and the poor kid has had such a hard life. Then he got involved with the wrong crowd. This week he was arrested for dealing cocaine, but I think I found an attorney who can get the charge dismissed. It will drain our savings, but I'll do anything to help him get through this.

"Sure, Tommy is twenty-four, but I really believe he will grow out of this stage. He's just in a rough place right now. He doesn't have a job, so he desperately needs me. I'll do anything to help him. I couldn't possibly turn my back on my own flesh and blood!"

Counselors and frustrated friends hear variations of these stories all the time. And some of them may be your own! Like Sarah and Janelle, most of us desperately want to help the people we love, but some relationships suck us in like quicksand—and before we know it, we're stuck . . . emotionally, financially, and perhaps even physically. If we express true love by saying "no more," we could unleash a horrible nightmare. If we draw a line in the sand and put boundaries in place, we can't control the outcome. The fear of the "what ifs" can overwhelm and paralyze us.

What kinds of craziness have you put up with or made excuses for . . . all in the name of "love"? Check all that apply to you. (It's okay, don't be shy—Pat and I [Tim] have been there too!)

- ❏ Keeping secrets
- ❏ Tolerating abuse
- ❏ Closing your eyes to irresponsible behavior
- ❏ Sacrificing to cover up someone else's mistakes
- ❏ Catering to a lazy person's whims
- ❏ Caving in to an angry person's demands
- ❏ Making excuses
- ❏ Justifying bad behavior
- ❏ Accepting the blame for something we never did
- ❏ Enabling an addiction
- ❏ Lying to yourself or others

In the name of love, we bail out people who won't help

themselves. Each time we insist, "This is the last time!" But it never is.

In the name of love, we endure name-calling, the silent treatment, temper tantrums, even violence. We try to assure ourselves, "Deep down he's a good person with a kind heart . . . he'll change." But he never really does.

In the name of love, we cower in the face of an angry person's demands and settle for whatever peace we can get. Which isn't much.

Why? What keeps us there? A misunderstanding of love.

What the world calls "love" often isn't true love at all. If our version of love is destroying us or someone we care about, then let's not call it love. There are lots of other names for it, but it's not love.

If that's you, if you or someone you know has been mistaking counterfeit love for the real thing, then you need a breakthrough—a flash of insight and a dose of courage to take action and change the status quo. And that's what this book will give you.

Change doesn't happen quickly or easily, but stick with us. Step by step, you can learn—and live—authentic love, wise trust, genuine forgiveness, and real freedom.

Snapshots of Crazy Love

While most of our relationships may be healthy and satisfying, we typically have one or two people who change the rules and get to us—a sibling, a spouse, son or daughter, coworker, boss, or close friend. These strained relationships drive us crazy, yet we seem to be helpless to exercise true love and move toward a more healthy relationship. Perhaps you will see a snapshot of yourself or a loved one in one of these examples:

• Bethany's husband, Rick, began acting a bit strangely a few years ago. Their sexual relationship became more intense, but less regular. She couldn't figure it out, and he didn't want to talk about it. One morning, Bethany opened Rick's computer and found a dozen porn sites he had viewed the night before. When she checked the history, she realized what he'd been doing all those nights he claimed to be "working late" before he came to bed. Rick got busted for visiting porn sites at work too.

Bethany and Rick's marriage was on the rocks. *I've been such a fool!* Bethany thought. *I should have known something like this was happening!*

She confronted Rick, but he insisted it was "no big deal" and "all the guys do it." When she didn't agree, he turned the tables, blaming her for not being sexually attractive enough.

He's right, Bethany reflected. *I have gained weight. If only I were as beautiful as I was on our wedding day. But I still do everything I can to please him sexually.*

Bethany had countless conversations with her closest friends to try to sort out her thoughts. But no matter what they said, Bethany insisted, "I know Rick loves me. It's my fault that we aren't where we should be. Yes, I know pornography is wrong, but it's what men do."

• Jackson and Susan were conscientious, attentive parents. They went to all of their son Bill's ball games and gave him plenty of guidance to stay out of trouble. When Bill went off to college, he made good grades, but he also made friends with a wild group of kids who partied every weekend.

A few years after Bill graduated from his master's program, they discovered he had been addicted to hydrocodone and Xanax since his junior year. "I knew he drank a lot," Jackson lamented to a counselor, "but I had no idea he was on drugs."

Bill had racked up huge debts, so Jackson and Susan brought him home to live with them. For two long years, they pleaded and threatened to get him to give up drugs. They did so much for him, but nothing worked. Several times, when Bill was really strung out, Jackson even called Bill's employer to tell him Bill was sick.

"I know it's wrong," Jackson defended himself when a friend questioned his actions, "but I can't let Bill lose his job. He would lose his health insurance and ruin his credit. It would devastate him, and I love him too much to let that happen to him. I just wish he would turn his life around."

• From the time her dad walked out the door, Rachel lived with her mother. But her mom was so emotionally distraught and overworked that she didn't have much left to help Rachel and her brother grow up. Rachel felt emotionally abandoned by both of her parents, and she grew to hate her mom. *Dad abandoned me once*, she thought to herself. *But mom abandons me every day.*

When Rachel got married and had a daughter of her own, she was determined to protect her from the pain she had endured. She smothered her daughter with attention—which was kind of cute when she was three, but a problem when she was fifteen. Rachel was consumed by wanting to know every detail of her daughter's life. She read all the postings on her daughter's Facebook page daily. After her daughter went to bed at night, Rachel looked through her schoolbooks to find notes her friends had sent her.

When Rachel told a friend what she was doing, the friend was alarmed. "You'll ruin your relationship with your daughter," the friend warned.

"To protect her, I have to know what's going on in her life," Rachel insisted. "I check my daughter's text messages, read her diary, and try to listen to every conversation she has on the phone. I've got to tell you, the things I've found out make my hair stand on end! She's in big trouble! I don't want her to make the same mistakes I made. I love her too much to let that happen!"

• On their first date, Kim and Jasper fell madly in love. They shared a common commitment to Jesus and enjoyed being together. Kim admired Jasper's strength and confidence. When they married the following year, everyone said it was a match made in heaven.

Soon after the honeymoon, however, Jasper began questioning the way Kim spent money. It wasn't that she was irresponsible—quite the opposite. She tried to explain that he could trust her, but that just made him angry and more demanding. He gave her mixed messages of tender affection and intense questions—probing accusations that were more like the cross-examination of an attorney than the inquiries of a loving spouse.

Kim realized that she had married a total control freak who treated her like a child. Jasper dominated her every moment and every action: How she folded the laundry, washed the dishes, and prepared the meals. Who she talked to on the phone. How she dressed and where she shopped. Even how much toilet paper she used! Seriously! He was breaking her down fast.

She began withdrawing emotionally and physically but felt guilty for not wanting to have sex with Jasper. He quoted a passage in 1 Corinthians about the wife's body belonging to her husband, but his use of Scripture didn't do a lot to promote feelings of intimacy. She felt dominated, falsely accused, and hopelessly trapped because no one outside their home had any idea what was going on. Most of her friends still thought it was a match made in heaven.

• From the time he was a little boy, James heard his dad—a pastor and highly respected man in the community—tell him, "People are watching you all the time because you're my son.

Make me proud, and make Jesus proud." But when he was in junior high, it seemed to James that his dad was more interested in his own reputation than how James' behavior reflected on Jesus.

Every night at dinner, his dad recited a litany of expectations: "I want the best for you, son. I want you to excel for the glory of God." But his dad's reaction to his failures told a different story. His dad employed the heavy guns of guilt and harsh condemnation instead of the gentle assurance of loving correction. The slightest infraction was severely punished, and even his friends' mistakes were viciously condemned. If James ever tried to protest, his dad became angry and violent: "Shut up, son. Shut up and do as you're told. One day you'll thank me for tough love."

At the end of each diatribe, his dad always said, "It's about doing God's work and being God's man." James wanted to live for God—he just felt so confused. His dad said he loved him, but then he lashed out in anger whenever James made a mistake. *Is God the same way?* he wondered.

James felt paralyzed to confront his dad about how much he was hurt. Any back talk was met with angry criticism. Over time, James grew to hate his dad, and eventually, God as well. The young man drifted into a deep depression, which greatly displeased his father, who continued to heap on the legalistic expectations. James felt trapped by his dominating dad and a seemingly disengaged and disinterested God.

Counterfeit Love

Truth be told, these snapshots don't just illustrate what crazy love looks like, they demonstrate counterfeit love. And though it may be easy for us to see its devastating impact in these stories, it's not so easy to see the truth when the story is our story.

When it comes to our most cherished relationships, we want to believe that the people we value really love us. We want to believe that we matter to them. That's just a part of our relational DNA. Most of the people we're close to—even the ones who are not loving us properly—do care about us in some fashion, but at the same time, they may care even more about themselves. Or they may simply not know how to love.

Regardless of the choices they make, *you* can learn the secrets to loving well. You can learn to recognize and receive real love when it comes your way—and push back when it doesn't. You can learn to really love the people in your life—and know when and how to help them. And that's what this book is for.

One-Up, One-Down

Difficult people distort our perceptions about love with:
- their pleas and demands ("If you really love me, you'll _____.")
- their threats ("If you don't _____, I'll leave you!")
- their spiritual accusations ("You call yourself a Christian?")

For Christians, our response is often complicated by sermons that emphasize:

- "Turn the other cheek."
- "Sacrifice like Jesus, who gave to the point of death."
- "Don't be selfish."
- "Honor and obey your parents."
- "Give, expecting nothing in return."
- "Don't let the sun go down on your anger."

While each of these statements is biblical, counterfeit love takes them out of context and so twists them around that they become nooses around our necks instead of guidelines to live by.

It's no wonder we often turn a blind eye to the truth that others plainly see!

Often, our misunderstandings about love are born in disruptive family relationships, where someone was either one-up or one-down to an extreme. There is an appropriate and necessary difference in the balance of power between parents and young children, but in the best situations, there should be no power struggles by the time those children have become adults—just deep connection, trust, and respect between people who sincerely care about each other.

In disruptive families, children are taught to remain one-up or one-down into adulthood. And this produces immature adults who either seek to dominate others (one-up) or who allow themselves to be dominated (one-down) in their relationships—one powerful and one needy, one enabling and one addicted, one decisive and one confused.

In relationships with these people, manipulation abounds. Especially when they start to feel out of control.

At the first hint of any threat to their security, dominant people will look to control others. Sometimes this expresses itself as you'd expect: pushiness, demands, insensitivity, and selfishness. But there are also dominant people who come disguised as helpers. They will naturally gravitate toward needy people—especially those who are most out of control—so they can "rescue" yet another soul, which makes them feel even more powerful.

For those in the one-down position, they'll either drift toward isolation when under pressure—avoiding relationships to protect themselves—or they'll lose themselves in someone else (enmeshment), letting that individual define their purpose, values, and desires.

People who tend to isolate don't feel safe, so their solution is to avoid meaningful interaction at all costs. To them, meaningful connection is a threat, because they define love as "no demands and no risks." Instead of experiencing a healthy connectedness with others, isolaters bounce off people like billiard balls. And usually everyone gets hurt, including the isolated one.

For those who are prone to enmeshment, they have almost no sense of identity apart from another person—and so, when someone "threatens" their overattachment with the desire for a healthy, interdependent relationship, they latch on all the more. Instead of being a distinct individual who shares ideas, love, and life with another distinct individual, the cling-on will opt for one messy entity—like two blobs of mud stuck together.

The term *enmeshment* was first popularized by Salvador Minuchin, who described it as "an extreme form of proximity and intensity in family interactions."[1] This uber-closeness produces weak boundaries and an inability to function as individuals, apart from the family. However, you can be enmeshed, or entangled, with anyone. It's not just for families!

Enmeshment creates codependent relationships—a dance, if you will—between two people that is "characterized by preoccupation with and extreme dependence (emotionally, socially, and sometimes physically) on a person or object."[2] Given enough time, this dependence on another person can become so rooted in our lives that it affects all other relationships.

Why Do We Keep Dancing?

Entangled relationships come in all shapes and sizes, but inevitably, one person takes the lead and dominates from a position of strength and authority, and the other complies from weakness and need in a toxic sort of tango. The weaker person constantly checks himself to see if his thoughts, attitude, and behavior will please (or at least avoid the wrath of) the dominant one, while the stronger person decides and dictates the life of the weaker one.

The great tragedy of being overly involved with someone is that you get caught up in a dance to make that person happy, and yet the dance leaves you empty-handed and broken-hearted, like a bad prom night.

So why do we keep dancing?

It's a family problem. Our early family relationships are extremely powerful. According to attachment theory (a fancy term for how we connect with other people), these relationships set the tone for the rest of our lives.

Our interactions with parents and primary caregivers during early childhood (particularly during the first two years) provide the answer to two critical questions about others and ourselves:

- Am I worthy of being loved?
- Are other people capable, willing, and available to love me?

Your behavior for the rest of your life will be deeply rooted in the answers to these questions. For when our families are encouraging, caring, and responsible, we learn how to love and be loved, and how to exercise proper limits along the way. On the other hand, when our families are dismissive, abusive, or smothering, we develop faulty beliefs about relationships that mess with our minds. We then take these beliefs and expectations into new relationships and keep repeating the same mistakes.

That's why enmeshment is so destructive and hard to eliminate. It's like a hidden cancer that eats away at the intimacy and true love God longs for us to enjoy. The crazy thing is, the one who holds control over us doesn't even have to be present! Even when they've moved away or died, the recording of our core relationship beliefs keeps running. In response, we constantly check our choices, seeking to align them with the approval of the person on whom we depend:

"Well, you know what Mom would say about that."

"Dad would roll over in his grave."

"My ex always criticized me when I did that."

"My old coach never would have let that slip."

UNDERSTANDING OUR CORE RELATIONSHIP BELIEFS

Below is a brief summary of the beliefs we hold about our relationships, and what those beliefs say about our level of attachment, or bonding, with the people we're closest to.[3] Take a moment to identify which "self" and "other" statements you identify with the most.

SECURE ATTACHMENT	AVOIDANT ATTACHMENT
Self Dimension • I'm worthy of love • I'm capable of getting the love I need *Other Dimension* • Others are willing and able to love me • I can count on you to be there for me	*Self Dimension* • I'm worthy of love (false pride) • I'm capable of getting the love I want and need (false sense of mastery) *Other Dimension* • Others are incompetent • Others are untrustworthy
AMBIVALENT ATTACHMENT	**DISORGANIZED ATTACHMENT**
Self Dimension • I am not worthy of love (I feel flawed) • I am unable to get the love I need without being angry or clingy *Other Dimension* • Capable but unwilling (due to my flaws) • May abandon me (due to my flaws)	*Self Dimension* • I am not worthy of love • I am unable to get the love I need *Other Dimension* • Others are unwilling • Others are unable • Others are abusive; I deserve it

Within these categories, the ambivalent and disorganized attachment styles are most likely to become enmeshed. Although we may not express these core beliefs out loud, they most certainly are woven into the fabric of our lives. They affect our every thought, relationship, choice, and goal in life.

The dancc may continue for generations in any number of settings: amid abuse, abandonment, the death of a parent, chronic disease, addiction, divorce, religious rigidity, and more. Anything that causes us to experience deep rumbles of insecurity can push us to the extremes of isolation or enmeshment, and the aftershocks are felt first and foremost within our families. This is why people who are two or three generations removed from a home environment that included an addict, an abuser, or someone with a mental disorder may still exhibit signs of isolation or entanglement.

Opening Our Eyes to the Truth

Thankfully, we don't have to stay there. We can push back and become happier, healthier people. It all begins with a flash of realization—a moment that changes everything.

I (Pat) grew up in an alcoholic home. My father was physically present but emotionally absent. My mother tried to cope with the strain and pain of life by controlling everything and everyone around her. She was a beautiful, bright, and gifted woman. People outside the family saw her as the perfect wife, perfect mother, and perfect club member. She couldn't control my father's drinking, so she devoted herself to controlling me.

Everything I did received my mother's detailed critical analysis: good or bad. She lavished praise when I did well, and she sharply corrected me when I deviated from her lofty expectations. As a young boy, I concluded that the best way to navigate these waters was to "read" my mother exceptionally well so I could change my behavior to suit her. Then I'd win her approval and escape her fierce eye and sharp tongue. She only exploded in rage a few times, but those awful moments became permanently embedded in my memory.

My mother dominated me, and I lost myself in her. When I was a teenager, I remained an extension of my mother. I continued to read her facial expressions so as to avoid condemnation and win approval. Mixed messages are incredibly manipulative, so I lived with a constant blend of fear and hope. I always feared her disapproval, but I always hoped to earn the love I desperately wanted.

Even after Joyce and I were married, my mother continued to tell us how we should live: how we should decorate our home, what kind of meals to cook, how to raise our children, how to vote, where to go on vacations, and on and on. When our children, Catherine and Taylor, were babies, the crushing weight of depression finally convinced me that I needed help. I began reading books and talking about my childhood experiences, and gradually I opened my eyes to the truth about my relationship with my mother and began to grow up emotionally.

When the kids were about six and seven years old, we went to visit my mother. The second day we were there, Joyce and I went out for an errand before lunch. When we came back, Catherine came up to us with a pained expression on her face. She asked, "Why does Kitty [her grandmother] have to tell me what to do all the time?"

Out of the mouths of babes! She had observed in an instant what took me thirty-five years to see.

The four of us went for a drive to talk about the morning's events. I explained, "When I was your age, your grandmother told me what to say, where to go, what to do, what to believe, and everything else." I could tell that my son, Taylor, was thinking hard. After a long pause, he said matter-of-factly, "So, Dad, when you were a kid, your mother was your brain." It was an accurate analysis. We laughed, but at that instant, I had a better grasp of the emotional, mental, and relational stranglehold my mother had exerted on me. My children had spoken truth!

From the outside, being so thoroughly attached may look good, but it's not true love. There is a fine line between being a loving mom and a dominating, controlling mom. We may call it love, but enmeshment is:

• smothering a weak, needy person with too much attention and direction

• giving in (meekly or defiantly) to the demands of a dominating person

• taking responsibility for another's choices instead of letting him experience the consequences of his decisions

• losing your identity in someone else, being dominated by them, and taking on that person's emotions, values, thoughts, and behaviors

• switching roles with your children and expecting them to meet your emotional needs

• building your relationship on power instead of mutual respect

Enmeshed relationships leave a legacy of heartache and manipulation. But that legacy can be changed if we are willing to open our eyes. One of the surest ways to uncover our over-involvement with someone is by asking the simple question, "How are you?"

When a counselor asked this question of Jackson and Susan (the parents of Bill in one of the "Snapshots of Crazy Love"), Jackson responded, "Well, Bill seems to be doing a little better this week." Susan nodded in agreement. The counselor didn't correct them, but he kept asking the same question each week to see if their response changed.

Finally, the counselor said, "When I ask you how you're doing, you always tell me about Bill—never about yourselves. What does that tell me?"

Jackson looked sheepish, but he finally got the point: "I guess we haven't really understood all you've been trying to tell us about being too involved in Bill's problems, have we?"

From that moment on, these two parents had a better understanding of how their addicted son had dominated their lives, and how they needed to respond: they would draw some boundary lines and let their son make his own choices. Choices that would force him to experience the consequences of his actions.

Misguided Devotion

To blindly persist in the dance of enmeshment is to continue down a destructive path. (Can't you hear Dr. Phil saying, "How's that working for ya?") Yet the devotion displayed between the powerful and the needy can appear endearing on the surface. In fact, we hear its seemingly charming phrases every day:

- "I'd die without you."
- "Without you, my life is empty."
- "You'd be nothing without me."
- "I can't do anything without you."
- "You make me whole."
- "You define me."
- "When I'm not with you, I'm hopelessly lost."
- "If you left me, I'd be nobody."
- "Where would you bc without me?"
- "Don't worry. I'll take care of you."

But being insecurely attached is lethal. When we define love as dominance ("I know what's best for him"), we feel completely justified in smothering people with too much attention and too much direction. And when we define love as compliance ("Yes, she can make my decisions better than I can"), we feel so utterly incompetent that we're happy to let the assertive person tell us how to live.

However, such misguided devotion doesn't satisfy us. It robs us of sanity, peace, joy, and the true love of a healthy relationship. Furthermore, entangled relationships produce tremendously powerful but conflicting emotions. The dominant individual may feel sorry for the weak one, but sooner or later (usually sooner), he resents and even despises the weak person's inability to cope with life. Initially, the weak person is grateful for the dominant one's help, but being treated like a child inevitably generates fierce anger. When these fiery emotions surface, the needy person is often caught by surprise and feels terribly ashamed: "How could I be angry at someone who has done so much for me?"

The story of Marianne and Rafe is a classic example.

From the time Rafe was born, Marianne devoted herself to her son. When his drinking became a problem, she invested herself in fixing every problem—and by the time he was an adult, there were plenty of them! He was married and divorced seven times, started and lost several businesses, was in and out of jail for drunk driving, and habitually got into trouble for tax evasion. Through it all, Marianne bailed him out—literally and figuratively. She constantly made excuses to others like, "Rafe can't help it"; "All his problems are just bad luck"; and "He is really a fine son."

Every time Rafe got into a jam, he would call his mom for help. One day, though, when he went to her house to pick up a check, she attacked him with the fury of a bobcat! She told him how disappointed she was in him and that this was the last time she would give him money. But he knew better; he could always count on another check.

How did these two feel about each other? One night when

he was drunk, Rafe told a friend, "My mother? I hate her. Hate her!" Now he was screaming. "I can't stand the way she treats me like a child! Someday, I'm going to have nothing to do with her—ever!"

And Marianne? She would tell herself, *Rafe loves me. He'll do anything for me.* Yet he never so much as bothered to pay her back more than a few token dollars when times were good.

Mother and son desperately needed each other, and had you asked, they would have defined their overly dependent relationship as love. Yet they couldn't mask the fact that they deeply despised each other.

Break Through to Freedom

It is possible to break the pattern of enmeshment and break through to freedom—to that place where we are able to give and receive true love. Our goal is not to find some kind of relational Nirvana where there are no problems, but to grow wise enough and strong enough to carve out our own identity. To be secure enough that we aren't compelled to control others or let them control us. To break free so that we can love with grace and truth as Jesus did.

The love Jesus offered was always open-handed and clear-eyed; it was never manipulative or deceptive. Jesus didn't lie to get people to do what he wanted them to do; he spoke the truth and offered a relationship based on trust and respect. Then he let people make their own choices. When they decided to follow him, he was pleased; when they walked away, he undoubtedly had tears in his eyes.

Jesus told his followers, "If you hold to my teaching, you are really my disciples. Then you will know the truth, and the truth will set you free" (John 8:31–32). In Galatians 5:1, Paul wrote, "It is for freedom that Christ has set us free."

When you discover how to live in love, the truth will set you free. Free to enjoy true, God-honoring love built on mutual understanding and intimacy. But first you'll have to expose your false perceptions of love to the light. When you do, everything in your world will be challenged to the core. But don't worry. Pat and I (Tim) will walk you through, step-by-step.

True love offers a safe place to be you; it's not driven by a desire to rescue or a need to perform. True love values the other person for who they are and celebrates healthy separateness.

By discovering God's plan for love and learning to live by it—exactly the things this book will help you accomplish—you can open the door to freedom from entangled relationships, find healing for your painful past, and gain the ability to love wisely and be loved in return.

THINK ABOUT IT . . .
....

1. How would you define and describe enmeshment in your own words?

2. Of the people you read about, with whom do you identify most closely? Explain your answer.

3. In what ways can enmeshment appear to be true love?

4. How can we discern the differences between enmeshment and authentic love?

5. What similarities do you see between entangled relationships and slavery? Is this a good analogy? Why or why not?

6. What do you hope to gain by reading this book?

CHAPTER 2

BREAK THROUGH TO TRUE LOVE

LET LOVE BE WITHOUT HYPOCRISY.

—*Romans 12:9 (NKJV)*

Before we can talk about the specifics of real love, we need to establish one overarching principle: *true love sees to love as Jesus loves.* Jesus' final command to his disciples was: "Love one another, as I have loved you" (John 13:34). How does Jesus love? Genuinely. Unselfishly. Radically. He laid down his life for us.

True love always expresses a willingness to lay down one's own life and desires for the benefit of another. That's why Paul challenged those who follow Jesus to "Do nothing out of selfish ambition or vain conceit, but in humility consider others better than yourselves. Each of you should look not only to your own interests, but also to the interests of others" (Philippians 2:3-4 NIV1984).

Of course we must be very careful here. There is a great

difference between the sacrificial selflessness of true love and the self-serving martyrdom of codependency. Jesus didn't go to the cross to feel "needed" or to meet a void in his life. His heart was motivated by obedience to his heavenly Father and a sincere love for each one of us.

Despite our best intentions, relationships in a fallen world aren't easy. Many of us are wired to manipulate and control rather than to genuinely cherish and honor others. When a person is so needy that he or she cannot stop "helping" someone else, it's not love. It's obligation. It's manipulation. True love, on the other hand, moves us from a place of saying, "I want to do something for you because it meets my needs," to "I want to do something for you because I love you."

Of course, we aren't Jesus, and we will never love perfectly. But what would it look like to love other people with the kind of love that Jesus so freely gave—with no ulterior motive or desire for something in return?

How, for example, does God want us to love an addict, a prodigal, or an abuser? If a demanding, angry, manipulative spouse or boss commands us to "submit," does love have to cower in fear as we obey? If a needy, irresponsible daughter or sibling asks to be bailed out financially over and over again, is it loving to "lord it over" that person so that we feel powerful? In order to love with the genuine love of Jesus, we must learn to answer two critical questions: When does true love give in? When does true love push back?

True Love Is Wise and Strong

Jesus admonished his followers to be "wise as serpents and harmless as doves" (Matthew 10:16 NKJV). This means we are to understand the dynamics of motives and actions in relationships. We also are to act with astute wisdom—motivated by true love, not a desire for manipulation or revenge. True love is strong enough to speak the truth and do what is best for someone else, even if that person doesn't like it. True love seeks wisdom to ensure that we're acting like mature, responsible adults instead of being doormats, compulsive fixers, or rage-aholics.

Some of us are in abusive relationships because we've been convinced that we don't deserve anything better. The abuser (and occasionally, a misguided Christian leader) may use the Bible to convince us that love would have us excuse and tolerate such behavior—that we have no right to self-protection. They insist that loving Christians have no rights at all.

In one sense, their claim is true. If we call Christ "Lord," we submit ourselves to his leading wherever he may direct us; we have no right to push back against the will of God. At the same time, God has given us the right and responsibility to act appropriately and justly in human relationships. As his beloved children, we are to love and to be strong and wise. This means there will be times when we need to push back.

When someone is abusing or controlling us, we are to protect ourselves. Paul warned Timothy about a man who had attacked him: "Alexander the metalworker did me a great deal of harm. The Lord will repay him for what he has done. You too should be on your guard against him, because he strongly opposed our message" (2 Timothy 4:14–15). We need to be on guard against those who have hurt us or who threaten to hurt us. We must be willing and ready to push back. But this doesn't mean we take revenge.

Are we to forgive those who have hurt us or continue to try to control us? Yes, God commands us to forgive them whether they say they are sorry and even if they don't change. That's because forgiveness allows us to release the heart! But should we continue to trust someone who continually hurts us? Not necessarily.

Forgiveness and trust are separate issues. It only takes one person to forgive, but two to reconcile. While God commands us to love and to forgive, we are never commanded to trust untrustworthy people. Trust must be earned by kind, respectful, consistent behavior. It is foolishness—not love—that compels us to give in by trusting those who haven't proven that they are trustworthy.

True Love Stands against Evil

Christians who have experienced oppressive or abusive relationships often believe that love means they need to turn the other cheek without even uttering a word of protest. After all, in his most famous sermon, Jesus told us,

You have heard that it was said, "Eye for eye, and tooth for tooth." But I tell you, do not resist an evil person. If anyone slaps you on the right cheek, turn to them the other cheek also. And if anyone wants to sue you and take your shirt, hand over your coat as well. If anyone forces you to go one mile, go with them two miles. Give to the one who asks you, and do not turn away from the one who wants to borrow from you. (Matthew 5:38–42)

The life of Jesus brings clarity here. He always stood against oppressors for the benefit of the hurting and the weak. He exposed the hypocrisy of powerful leaders. Again and again, he resisted evil people. It's true that at the trials before his execution he "did not open his mouth" to defend himself, but at that point, his purpose was to go to the cross and die to pay for the sins of the world. In every other instance, Jesus was a tireless defender of the helpless, and he defended himself against attacks (for example, see John 5:16–47).

When Jesus told us not to resist an evil person, he meant for us to avoid violence in our resistance. And when people offend us, it's appropriate to give them the benefit of the doubt by "turning the other cheek," "walking a second mile," and "handing over our coat." How many times are we to do this? Enough to show that we aren't engaging in retribution.

Many of us, though, have been turning our cheeks, walking for miles, and handing over our coats thousands of times just to avoid confronting the evil around us. Commentators such as John Calvin have even gone so far as to say that it is inappropriate to turn the other cheek if this choice would confirm the other person in a pattern of sin. Calvin wrote, "I admit that Christ restrains our hands, as well as our minds, from revenge: but when any one has it in his power to protect himself and his property from injury, without exercising revenge, the words of Christ do not prevent him from turning aside gently and inoffensively to avoid the threatened attack."[1]

And we must not forget that many of us have been on the giving end of controlling behavior. We've smothered those we claim to love, or we've made demands to direct their behavior. To stand up for true love in such relationships requires heartfelt apologies and a sincere offer to rebuild the relationship on renewed trust and respect.

True Love Is Rooted in God's Love

A weak, misguided definition of love causes us to give in repeatedly, but a stronger, more accurate view of love directs us to speak and act wisely to address evil, manipulative behavior. Rather than just "taking anything," we can begin to check ourselves. We can invite Jesus into what we're experiencing and gain a new approach to love and biblical limits. We can ask, "Lord, please show me your love. I know that too often my attempts to love fall way short. How would you want me to respond here? Is giving in enabling this person?

Show me my true motives for wanting to jump in and help or control. I know it is your job—not mine—to fix and heal others. Show me how to genuinely and sincerely love this person. Give me courage to be honest, take appropriate responsibility, and trust wisely . . ."

As we grapple with these tough questions, we must bring our hearts and minds back to the fundamental, unchanging truth of God's love for each one of us. That's why Paul wrote, "And I pray that you, being rooted and established in love, may have power, together with all the saints, to grasp how wide and long and high and deep is the love of Christ, and to know this love that surpasses knowledge—that you may be filled to the measure of all the fullness of God" (Ephesians 3:17–19 NIV1984).

Rooted. Grounded. Established. Having power. Filled to overflowing. When we choose to live in God's love—to root and ground our hearts in the reality of the Cross—insecurity, doubt, and fear begin to lose their hold. In their book *Love is a Choice*, Robert Hemfelt and Frank Minirth point out, "With [God's] love encompassing you, you need no longer tie yourself in the codependent knots of an unhealthy relationship, grasping, enmeshing, suffocating, and being suffocated. 'The truth shall make you free,' said Jesus in John 8:32. Free! Free to enjoy, free to choose. And one of the choices is love."[2]

True love is not wrapped up in a drive to rescue, overprotect, control, or manipulate. It genuinely wants the best for the other person. It is grounded in our heart's desire to cherish, honor, and treasure another person simply because of who they are. This kind of love enables us to see people as Jesus does—to be moved by affection, devotion, and genuine care. It's not preoccupied with indulging someone's wants or feeling indispensible.

True Love Will Not Fail

Learning to "love like Jesus" takes practice . . . and a whole lot of grace. Growth and change take time. In his insightful book *After You Believe*, N. T. Wright observes that genuine transformation isn't just following a set of rules or hoping change will magically happen.[3] Instead, spiritual and emotional maturity occur gradually by the beautiful blend of the Holy Spirit's work and our diligent effort to acquire new knowledge and skills. Wright compares this process to learning a new language or mastering a musical instrument or sport.

We can't expect to fly into a foreign land and suddenly speak the native language fluently. We have to do the painstaking work of learning the vocabulary, conjugating the verbs, and practicing our pronunciation. At first, the new language seems very awkward and difficult, but if we stay with it, the language becomes second nature, and speaking with people from that culture becomes richly rewarding. In the same way, we may not know which end of a tennis racquet or violin bow to hold at first, but with diligence and proper training, we learn to play with proficiency.

The language of true love may at first be foreign to our ears, but it satisfies the hunger of our hearts. The love God longs for us to experience in our relationships with others is described beautifully in this paraphrase of 1 Corinthians 13:

> Love is patient, but love is not passive. Love is kind, but not conniving. Love does not envy or boast—love is sincere. Love is not proud, rude, or self-seeking, but love is also not becoming a doormat. Love is not easily angered, but love is honest about disappointment, frustration, and even anger.
>
> Love keeps no record of wrongs, but love is also not a victim. Love does not delight in evil, and love also does not perpetuate evil by enabling an addict or abuser. Love rejoices in the truth and communicates the truth, because where the truth is, there is freedom. Love always protects, but love does not rescue or control.
>
> Love always trusts, but is also wise in who to trust. Love always hopes, but places that hope in Jesus Christ, not the approval of others. Love always perseveres, but love does not mean losing yourself.
>
> Love never fails, because it is not fueled by human strength. True love is rooted and grounded in God's unconditional love, not the need to fix or control someone else.[4]

Never Give Up!

Our perspective on love makes a world of difference. Every difficult person, every strained relationship, and every awkward conversation is a test, and God is the teacher. His purpose isn't to cause us to flunk. He wants to use each test to reveal himself and instruct us in what it means to truly love.

When we face these tests, we can find a hundred reasons to quit, but with tenacity and courage, we will find a way to keep moving forward. Ultimately, the only real failure is to give up. Those who make it are the ones who have a "whatever it takes" attitude to overcome their tangled relationships. Each day they find the strength and courage to try again, much like the select number of brave men and women who climb the most treacherous mountain peaks in the world. They don't climb for fame or fortune. They climb to challenge themselves to reach for more than they've ever achieved before. To push past the limits of physical and psychological endurance. To stare fear in the face—and take one more step.

At the young age of twenty-one, Stacy Allison caught the bug.[5] On her first major climb on Mt. Huntington in Alaska, she was only two hundred feet from the summit when her partner's ice ax broke. They turned around that day, brokenhearted but even more determined to reach the top of as many peaks as possible. And her attitude after that experience? "Our ability to respond positively to setbacks fuels our creativity and lays the foundation for future successes."[6]

The next year, Stacy reached the top of Mount McKinley, the tallest mountain in North America, and she participated with a team of women who climbed Nepal's Ama Dablam. These feats, though, were preparation for her assault on Mount Everest. She joined the North Face Expedition, but her team got caught in a storm and was trapped for five days in a snow cave above 23,000 feet. Having exhausted many of her resources, Stacy did not reach her goal on that day either, but she learned an important lesson about the value of tenacity. She returned to Mount Everest with the Northwest American Everest Expedition, and after climbing for twenty-nine days, she became the first American woman to reach the top of the world.

People who want to climb the world's highest mountains face months or years of conditioning, securing resources, and finding assistance to ascend the mountain. Those who make it to the top endure many moments of self-doubt. Still, they aren't willing to quit, no matter how many setbacks they face.

The lessons Stacy Allison learned in climbing apply to our emotional and spiritual journeys too. Relearning relationships requires similar grit and preparation. But the view from the top is stunning. What's more, each step of the journey is its own reward. And it's all in the name of true love. Real love.

When we have a realistic view of the process, we aren't shocked or too discouraged when we trip and fall down on the trail. We just get up, dust ourselves off, and ask God for grace to take another step. David's gut-honest cry becomes our own:

"When I thought, 'My foot slips,' your steadfast love, O Lord, held me up" (Psalm 94:18 ESV).

In the lifelong process of discovering what true love is, God's steadfast love holds us up. He will never leave us or forsake us along the way. And the more we experience and live in his love, the more we'll be free to love like him—with no strings attached, without demanding compliance or running away, and . . . without hypocrisy.

THINK ABOUT IT . . .

1. How would you describe what it means to love as Jesus loves?

2. In what situations can it be loving to push back and not give in to what another person wants from you? How do you decide when it is appropriate to push back or give in?

3. What have you thought it means to "turn the other cheek"? After reading this chapter, how have your views changed?

4. How real and vivid is God's love for you? In what ways do you need a more personal understanding of him?

5. Why is it essential to have a "whatever it takes" attitude toward the lessons of love?

CHAPTER 3

WHERE'S THE PAYOFF?

NOW THAT YOU HAVE PURIFIED YOURSELVES BY
OBEYING THE TRUTH SO THAT YOU HAVE SINCERE
LOVE FOR EACH OTHER, LOVE ONE ANOTHER
DEEPLY, FROM THE HEART.

—*1 Peter 1:22*

Helping others has always been its own reward. It brings a sense of purpose and meaning to our lives. It makes us feel good. And we may even feel a bit of a "high" when we can make a difference for someone. James, a graduate student in counseling, hinted at this intoxicating feeling when his friend asked how he could serve so selflessly and tirelessly.

"It's easy," James responded. "When I help somebody, I feel alive! When I'm needed, I know I'm somebody. Solving somebody's problems gives me a reason to live!"

There's certainly nothing wrong with extending compassion to those in need and sacrificing to serve others. When done with a full heart and no strings attached, these kindnesses are beautiful demonstrations of love. But when done to fill an empty heart that requires appreciation as the payoff, it's not love; it's manipulation.

Imagine if Jesus had taken this approach with the ten lepers. "You have a choice: I'll heal you, if and only if you tell me thanks; or else, forget it—no healing for you!" It's obvious how wrong this would be, and yet many of us approach others this way more often than we'd like to admit.

The Feel-Good Payoff

By this point in the book, you can probably detect an underlying motivation in James' motivation for helping others. He can't see anything wrong with it because his boundaries are blurred. Yet some of his closer friends sense that something isn't quite right. They have noticed that he gets a little too excited when his service is applauded, and a little too discouraged when no one seems to notice. That's one of the signs of enmeshment.

Whether they're: 1) stepping in to rescue someone who's in trouble, 2) telling someone else how to live their life, or 3) letting a dominant person dictate what they do each waking moment, virtually all enmeshed people believe they're doing the right thing. It not only feels right, but it comes with a big payoff.

For the dominant person, their payoff is that rush of adrenaline—the genuine buzz they get—from jumping in to fix problems. (One clue to discerning whether you're crossing the line from helping to overhelping is in your response to the size of the problem. Small problems usually aren't good enough for one-up fixers. They only feel good about themselves when they solve a real crisis. Their mantra is not just: "If there's a problem, I'll find a solution," but "The bigger the problem, the better!" If they face a small problem, they'll inflate it so that it looks bigger. Then they'll feel better about themselves because they are so indispensable!) The weak person's payoff, on the other hand, is a release of responsibility. They may also develop an intoxicating sense of importance and invincibility, believing others will always rush to their rescue. *When the wheels come off in my life, someone will come through for me, they think. Those who love me always do.*

Kate and her son Edward demonstrate the power of the payoff. Edward started smoking dope when he was in junior high, and by the time he was in college, he was drinking heavily and smoking crack. Whenever Kate talked about Edward, she'd always tell people he was "doing great!" even though he was constantly in debt, continually betraying the few friends he had, and persistently in and out of jail—and several jobs. It was puzzling to Kate's friends who knew otherwise. However, what they didn't understand was that she was on the stratospheric helper's high that is so symptomatic of enmeshed relationships.

You see, the arrangement between Edward and Kate was simple: he would create the chaos that fueled Kate's life, and Kate would step in like a superhero and rescue her son. The lower he sank, the more important and empowered she felt.

Kate sacrificed most of her money, an enormous amount of time, and her reputation with her friends for an irresponsible son who was more than happy to take everything she would give him. She sometimes ranted at Edward for being "so idiotic," but she never met a problem in his life that she wasn't ready to fix. She'd even lie awake at night worrying over Edward's current predicament and yet fantasizing about ways to help him.

Kate lived to solve Edward's problems. Each time he called, she'd bail him out. And with each bailout, Kate felt the heady rush of being needed. She got the payoff of knowing that he was still dependent on her; he got another free pass: no consequences. And with each cycle of need and fixing, their relationship became more entangled.

Though Edward hated being pitiful and needy, and he resented his mother for constantly treating him like a child, he did nothing to change because the status quo worked so well. As long as Mom was around, he would never have to take responsibility for his choices.

Feedback Fuels the Chaos

Throughout life, our choices are reinforced (or not) by the "feedback" we get from two primary sources: the consequences of our actions and the response of people we respect.

On the positive side, both our drive to succeed and our relationships at work are strengthened when the boss credits our team's wise planning and creative innovations for increasing company sales. In a family environment, treating people with respect, telling the truth, and being responsible for our choices creates a positive, wholesome atmosphere where everyone can relax, enjoy each other, and learn from their failures.

In enmeshed families and organizations, it's just the opposite. Feedback is as poisonous as a hose pumping carbon monoxide into a closed container—it continually pollutes the atmosphere.

The enmeshed version of feedback may include:

- blaming others
- minimizing unhealthy or sinful conduct
- obsessive worries about a floundering person
- unrealistic expectations (too high or too low)
- demands or a lack of communication instead of honesty
- smothering
- playing the victim

All such feedback leads to a confusing environment where

the powerful feel more necessary and the needy feel more helpless.

On the rare occasion that someone from the outside speaks truth to anyone in the enmeshed circle, the hearer has a choice: to accept the input or to discount it and crawl back into the cave of denial. Enmeshed people carefully filter the feedback of others and only listen to whatever fits with what they already believe.

For example, a supermom like Kate will accept accolades for being noble and generous. When she hears these praises, you can almost see her glow with pride! But if someone suggests that by making decisions Edward ought to make, Kate is actually harming her son, Supermom comes to her own defense: "You don't understand; I'm doing this for his own good. And if I didn't do it, who would? No one else is Edward's mother!"

In a similar way, Edward filters the input of others through his mother's twisted view of reality. "Why wouldn't she take care of me this way? I deserve the help she gives me. Who else is gonna do it? I can't do what she does for me."

The Fantasy Payoff

Both the dominant person and the needy person often live in highly dramatic fantasy worlds. The dominant one may daydream about being the hero who comes to the victim's rescue—sometimes at great harm to himself—to show how far he'll go to help those in need. The needy one has dreams too. She may envision a knight riding in on a white horse to swoop her up and carry her away to a life of love and leisure, or he may imagine winning the lottery and becoming a multimillionaire who never has to be concerned about the financial consequences of his decisions. The fantasy images of power and rescue have a strong impact on the expectations of the superhero and the victim, further entrenching both people in their rigid patterns and identities.

From the outside looking in, it appears that a change in certain patterns could break the cycle. We might want to shout, "Don't you see what you're doing? Just stop it!" But it isn't that easy. Not only do life experiences provide the payoff that enmeshed people desire, but even the way the brain works feeds the cycle.

Betrayed by Our Brains

Robert is a competent, respected structural engineer who feels helpless when dealing with his wayward son. "I'm an engineer. I fix stuff," he lamented. "All day every day, I analyze problems and find solutions. I'm good at what I do; the buildings I design stand tall and strong. But in my relationship with Josh, my brain goes dead or races ahead in worry. I can't seem to find anything that helps either him or me!"

His problem is amazingly common. Respected men and women who exhibit great intelligence and professional competence feel hopeless and act helpless in their most important relationships. Like Robert, they become paralyzed with obsessive worry or numbness. They may be astute managers in other areas of their lives, but in these key relationships, everything seems adrift in a fog of confusion. They feel unable to think clearly and make good choices. They keep doing the same things over and over again, hoping it will all turn out differently, but nothing ever changes.

Why are the minds of normally bright, decisive people reduced to mush when they face the problems of enmeshed relationships? It is because their brains are hardwired that way. That's right, your habits—from the things you do to the ways you think—make your brain functions fixed and rigid. In other words, good habits hardwire the brain to keep doing good things, and bad habits have the opposite effect. So changing the patterns of enmeshed relationships is a bit like driving on a road with deep ruts in hardened mud. We may try to avoid the ruts that have been carved by previous drivers—but it will make for a bumpy ride. And no matter how hard we try to steer a new course, we will slip into the same old ruts at times.

We all crave affection and affirmation, but when our brain structures or our brain chemistry are not functioning properly, we often seek affirmation from people who are irresponsible and untrustworthy. We confuse love with worry and enabling behavior, and we develop rigid but unproductive patterns of thinking and acting. It's even possible to get locked in to pessimistic beliefs, convinced that nothing will ever work out. Eventually, we may develop an emotional paralysis called *learned helplessness*, in which we believe that all options are gone and we have no choices.[1] In these situations, it's easy to remain stuck in the rut of existing habits—harmful as they might be— because we simply can't envision life any differently. We have tunnel vision, seeing only one way to act.

Superheroes Die Hard

Enmeshed people may feel indispensable for a long time, but sooner or later, they'll come across someone in need who they just can't rescue. Or, just as painful, they'll serve and give self-lessly, but the people for whom they make such great sacrifices don't appreciate them as much as they expected. Either way, they fall from their high pedestal with a resounding thud!

In some cases, the fallen superhero will adopt a new mantra: "People desperately need me, but I can't help them. I tried and failed, so I'm no good to anybody. Every time I try to help, I mess things up. But that's over now anyway. Nobody will ever ask for my help again!" Still, the superhero wants to live, and enmeshed people will pay a high price emotionally and physically to pursue the payoff.

Sally rode a roller coaster of emotions as she struggled with her success and failure as a savior. When she stepped in to fix her daughter's problems, she felt great, but when her advice was rejected or proved wrong, she felt worthless. Her feelings of despair, however, didn't open a window on her real problem. Sally simply concluded that she had to do a better job of fixing her daughter's problems next time!

Like most people who play the superhero role, Sally's compulsion to solve people's problems wasn't limited to her daughter's life. She constantly looked for needs among her extended family, her circle of friends, the women's ministry at church, and in her neighborhood. She would have been thrilled if someone she didn't even know called to ask for her help! That coveted call would confirm that she was valued and desired—which is what her service and advice-giving was all about anyway.

Some Sallys never get off the roller coaster. Should a friend dare to speak the truth or question their motives, they move on to other relationships and keep doing what they've always done. Others, however, actually allow the truth to change them.

Jonathan had volunteered in his church for a decade and, like Sally, he took his superhero role very seriously: he felt a heavy burden to meet the needs of the many people he encountered at work and in ministry, not to mention his family and friends. After watching Jonathan struggle under the load for a long time, a friend of his with great insight (Steve) told him, "I think you're taking yourself way too seriously. You don't have to carry the weight of the world on your shoulders."

Jonathan later told Steve that he had wanted to sarcastically respond, "Just because people don't come to you for help and advice, Sir Stevie, don't nag on me. Maybe we're not talking about me here, but you!" Instead, Jonathan said, "Oh, it's not a problem. I enjoy all that I do."

Steve shot back, "Then why do you look so burned out?"

To Jonathan, Steve had stepped over the line. "I don't!"

Steve smiled and said, "You know, we can act like we're in the third grade, but let's not. I'm telling you that I see a flaw—yes, a flaw—in your life. You're too invested in all this service. I know you love God; I'm not questioning that. But when someone can't say no, there's a deeper problem. That's all I'm saying. Just think about it."

Jonathan left fuming, but within a day or so, he realized that Steve was right. Helping others wasn't the problem, but his motive for doing so was out of balance. He called Steve to apologize, and after they talked for a while, he confessed, "I really have no clue how to lighten up. Everything I do seems more important than the things that really should matter."

"That, my friend, is a problem," Steve told him.

Gradually, Jonathan began to realize that his behavior had been compulsive, not noble—and certainly not normal. He also now understood that the payoff of praise no longer compensated for the price he was paying in fatigue, resentment, and increasing distance in every important relationship—including his relationship with God.

When the Light Breaks Through

In spite of overwhelming evidence that something needs to change, enmeshed people of both stripes—the powerful as well as the needy—continue to engage in the tiring dance of compulsive fixing and helpless passivity. Why? Why do so many of us keep pursuing the short-lived payoffs of applause and an adrenaline rush when plenty of signs point to the fact that our compulsive behaviors are, in fact, destroying us?

The answer is really quite simple: we're thoroughly convinced that what we are doing is the only way life works. But sometimes a single insight, a single ray of truth, breaks through and—perhaps for the first time—we can see that there may be a better payoff. One that can last a lifetime.

That one insight can begin a monumental change for the better.

Phil grew up in an alcoholic home full of anger and uncertainty. He was never sure how his parents would respond to any situation. One or both of them might erupt over something meaningless . . . or act as if nothing happened when a genuine tragedy occurred. At an early age, Phil's brother began to numb his pain with alcohol and drugs, but Phil tried desperately to please his parents and relieve some of the tension in the family.

Phil lived to make his mother happy most of all. The ever-attentive son, he was an expert at reading her facial expressions so that he could adjust his words and actions to please her. After he married and had children, Phil still thought about his mother every day. Even though his mother lived five hundred miles away, their relationship became a wedge between Phil and his wife. Fortunately, Phil got the professional help he needed to save his marriage and his family—thanks to his "moment that changed everything."

When Phil was growing up, he swore to himself and to God that he would never treat his children the way his mother had treated him. But one day, when his children were very young, he exploded at them in anger and demanded compliance or else! Suddenly, the brilliant light of truth flashed in his heart. He realized that as much as he didn't want to, he had become what he dreaded: a volatile parent.

When he saw in his kids' eyes the same terror that he had felt when he was a kid, it was forever seared in Phil's mind and heart. The truth shattered him, but out of the broken pieces came a rock-solid commitment to change. The payoff of enmeshment wasn't worth it. Whatever it took, however long it required, and no matter how many resources had to be invested, Phil resolved to find a way to change. It was that important.

As Phil instinctively realized, we can't undo the past. But we can shape the future for our children, our spouse, and ourselves. And so Phil was determined to change the only one he could possibly change: himself. He wanted to break the cycle of heartache and manipulation that could be traced back several generations in his family. He wanted to establish a new legacy for his wife and children based on truth, trust, and genuine love. He wanted a different and healthier payoff for his family. He wanted a true and lasting breakthrough. And he is on that course still today.

We'll read more of his journey in the coming chapters.

THINK ABOUT IT . . .

1. In what ways have enmeshed people lost the power to choose, and how is this like being relationally "stuck" in adolescence?

2. Why is it foolish to give in to an abuser, trust a liar, and be emotionally vulnerable to someone who has a compulsion to control you? What kind of damage does it do to you and your relationship with that person?

3. How do you think setting appropriate boundaries and taking appropriate responsibility help us to love more sincerely?

4. What do you feel are the most difficult or painful risks we face when we seek to make changes and "grow up" in our most important relationships?

5. What relationship changes do you most look forward to as you anticipate becoming a person who can do relationships well?

CHAPTER 4

ANSWER THE WAKE-UP CALL

MAN'S EXTREMITY IS GOD'S OPPORTUNITY.

—Thomas Adams

An alarm isn't a gentle summons; it's a jarring call to action, designed to get our attention. It warns us that something in life is out of control. Whether the house is on fire, the car door is open, or we need to get out of bed to go to work, an alarm alerts us to the risk we face if we continue unaware and unchanged.

In life, God graciously sounds the alarm to wake us up when we are overly involved in key relationships. However, we usually have another term for these alarms: *crisis*. A crisis screams, "Life's not working! Something's got to change!"

These moments are God's wake-up calls. They break through the fog and get our attention. They provide a window of clarity to help us see the truth about our lives and relationships. They can be the moments that change everything.

But very few of us change until we have to. Even when a crisis demands change, many of us hit the snooze button, bury our heads beneath the covers, and hope the moment will pass. It won't. We may convince ourselves that maintaining the status quo—enabling an addict, overindulging a child, losing ourselves in the needs of another, or believing an abuser's lies—are entirely normal. They aren't.

Thanks to his grace, God doesn't give up easily—he gives us many wake-up calls. It may take years for the most courageous of us to muster the inner strength to answer the alarm, but when we do, the true transformation of our relationships awaits!

Heed the Alarm

Alarms are intended to spur us into immediate, lifesaving action. Yet people who wouldn't consider staying in a building when the fire alarm goes off will stay in an enmeshed relationship after numerous wake-up calls. We might have experienced the heartache of divorce, financial collapse, depression, verbal or physical abuse, or a host of physiological problems caused by off-the-chart anxiety. Still, some of us find compelling reasons to stay in the burning building.

Catherine chose to ignore the alarms. She was married to a "functional alcoholic" who drank every day. Paul had been a successful businessman until the market collapsed and he lost his business. Then he drank more to numb his fear and shame. In a short time, he became an emotional recluse, retreating to an isolated world of scotch and television sports.

Catherine was furious. She could hardly believe that her family's financial situation had reversed so quickly. In just a few months, she had gone from diamonds and luxury cars to impending bankruptcy. She struggled to keep face, but for the first time since she was a teenager, she had to get a job to support the family.

During this awkward and explosive time, their son and daughter were adolescents. Fifteen-year-old William followed his father's example and began drinking heavily. Thirteen-year-old Michelle tried as hard as she could to please her mother. She saw how much stress her mother was under and couldn't understand why her dad and brother were so selfish. (That's the complaint her mother often voiced, and to Michelle it seemed like a good explanation.)

Eventually Paul got a job, but his spirit was broken. He was no longer the bold entrepreneur, husband, or father he had been. Their son, William, became a classic alcoholic: drifting from job to job and marriage to marriage, chronically out of money, and never at fault for anything that happened to him. Through it all, Catherine remained blindly devoted to her husband and son. Ten years after William graduated from college, Catherine was still "helping" him. She'd call him several times a day, and if she didn't call, he'd call her. He depended on his mother for advice and she gladly gave it.

Michelle wasn't as needy as William or her dad, so she became the odd person out. She tried very hard to connect with her mother, but realized that she was valuable to her mom only when she was involved in fixing William's problems. When Michelle realized she was just a pawn in the sick game played by her mother and brother, she backed out. This made her the object of scorn from the entire family. "How can you be so selfish?" they each scolded in their own way.

WHY WE HIT THE SNOOZE BUTTON

We may hit the snooze button and stay in unhealthy relationships for a variety of reasons. Some of these include:

- Fear of being alone—"I'd rather be with him/her than nobody at all."
- Loss of identity/purpose—"I won't know who I am anymore."
- Comfort—"It's all I've ever known."
- Resistance to change—"I'm pretty set in my patterns. I was born this way."
- Finances—"I can't survive on my own."
- Minimizing the problem—"Every relationship has some drama. Nobody's perfect."

- Desire to fix/control—"He/she can't survive without me."
- Living as a victim—"Since my family did this to me, they are responsible for fixing it."
- Faulty religious beliefs—"God commands me to love and give unselfishly, even when I lose myself in the process."
- Hopelessness—"It's too late for me. I'm stuck."

....

As you might imagine, this family had dozens of wake-up calls over the years. An alcoholic husband and son didn't get Catherine's attention. Neither did the bankruptcy of Paul's company. Paul didn't heed the alarms of liver disease and eventually died from complications of his addiction. William experienced an almost continuous alarm that his life was a disaster. Multiple divorces, DUIs, getting fired, and alcohol-related health problems not only should have been enough to get his attention, but should have caused Catherine to realize that her efforts to help her son were counterproductive too. Still, Catherine forged ahead.

"He can't do anything about it," she told an incredulous friend. "He's just like his father. And besides, I love him, and I can't let anything bad happen to him. No one else—including his sister—is willing to help him like I am."

Until the day she died, Catherine continued to excuse William's behavior, give him all her money, and alternately console him and fuss at him. She was never willing to face the painful reality that their absorbing, consuming, enmeshed relationship was ruining both of their lives. She hit the snooze button every time the alarm sounded.

It's Time to Wake Up

Daughter Michelle's version of this story, though, is different. For years she watched her family implode. She heard dozens of alarms that something drastic needed to change, and for a long time she followed her mother's example of minimizing and excusing the irresponsible behavior of the men in the family. But in her mid-thirties, the stress from trying to be her mother's assistant hero grew too great. She became clinically depressed—barely able to get up each day—which put her career in jeopardy.

But one day she heard the wake-up call, and she was ready. That was her breakthrough.

With the help of her doctor and counselor, Michelle discovered that she had been living with a crushing weight of repressed hurt, fear, and anger. This was another wake-up call for her. Would she move into the pain to resolve it so she could be free—or would she, like everyone else in her family, retreat into the stupor of denial?

Michelle was listening. With the encouragement of a friend, she chose to answer the alarm and break through into the light of reality. It was a pivotal moment in her life. Later, she remembered, "I wish I had noticed all those times before when a crisis brought me to a point of change, but I never realized what was going on. I'm glad, though, that I finally got the picture."

How Are You?—A Self-Test

So what's going on in your life? Do you, like Michelle, need to hear the wake-up call? What will it take for you to open your eyes to what is happening in your heart and your relationships? The following self-test may help you to see the picture more clearly. For each statement below, indicate your agreement or disagreement.

1. I am in a significant relationship with someone who is addicted to a substance or a behavior, someone who is depressed, or someone who is very needy. *Yes___ No___*

2. I often feel the weight of responsibility for others' happiness and well-being. *Yes___ No___*

3. I can't say no without feeling guilty. *Yes___ No___*

4. I can accurately "read" other people by analyzing their facial expressions and tone of voice. *Yes___ No___*

5. When I am able to fix others' problems, I feel strong and important. *Yes___ No___*

6. I feel that I have to protect people, especially the addicted, out-of-control, or depressed person in my life. *Yes___ No___*

7. I live in such a way that no one can ever say I'm selfish. *Yes___ No___*

8. I vacillate between defending the irresponsible person and blowing up in anger at him or her. *Yes___ No___*

9. I often relive situations and conversations to see if there's some way I could have done more or spoken better. *Yes___ No___*

10. I feel very frightened by angry people. *Yes___ No___*

11. I am quite offended by personal criticism. *Yes___ No___*

12. To avoid feeling guilt and shame, I seldom stand up to people who disagree with me. *Yes___ No___*

13. I tend to see people and situations as "all good" or "all bad." *Yes___ No___*

14. Though I try to please people, I often feel isolated and alone. *Yes___ No___*

15. I trust people too much or not at all. *Yes___ No___*

16. I often seek to get people I love to change their attitudes and behavior. *Yes___ No___*

17. I tend to believe the addicted or depressed person's promises, even if he or she has broken countless promises before. *Yes___ No___*

18. Sometimes I have a lot of energy to help people, but more often, I feel drained, depressed, and ambivalent. *Yes___ No___*

19. I frequently give advice, even when it isn't requested. *Yes___ No___*

20. I tend to confuse love with pity, and to love those who need me to rescue them from their problems. *Yes___ No___*

21. I believe I can't be happy unless others—especially the needy people in my life—are happy. *Yes___ No___*

22. I am often a victim in strained and broken relationships. *Yes___ No___*

23. I am looking for somebody who will love me completely and unconditionally. *Yes___ No___*

24. My thoughts are often consumed with the troubles and needs of the addicted or depressed person in my life. *Yes___ No___*

25. I feel wonderful when I can fix others' problems, but I feel terrible when I can't. *Yes___ No___*

Total: Yes___ No___

—If you answered yes to four or fewer statements, you probably have relatively healthy boundaries, confidence, and wisdom in relationships. You can care about people without feeling responsible for their choices.

—If you answered yes to five to twelve statements, your life is shaped to a significant degree by the demands of needy people in your life. You often feel responsible for the choices others make, and you try too hard to help them make the right ones. You would benefit from the input of a competent counselor or support group.

—If you answered yes to thirteen or more statements, you have lost your sense of identity, and you are consumed by the problems of addicted or depressed people in your life.

You believe you can't be happy unless you are rescuing irresponsible people from their destructive decisions. In reality, however, your hope for sanity and emotional health is not in that person getting well. You have to take steps to get well whether that person does or not. Find a counselor or a support group to help you gain wisdom and strength.

Every Alarm Is a Test

Once we, like Michelle, get the picture and decide to respond to the wake-up call, the really hard work begins. Alarms invite us to chart a new direction for life—a change in the way we think, in the way we act, and in the way we love those in our most important relationships—and nothing short of that. Making that change can be scary. It is gut-wrenching, hard work. No wonder we've opted for the snooze button so many times in the past!

Consider the work God's servant, Abraham, had to do when he responded to God's wake-up call. You know the story. God appeared to Abraham when he was seventy-five and promised to make him "a great nation" of countless descendants:

> Go from your country, your people and your
> father's household to the land I will show you. I
> will make you into a great nation, and I will bless
> you; I will make your name great, and you will be
> a blessing. I will bless those who bless you, and

whoever curses you I will curse; and all peoples on earth will be blessed through you. (Genesis 12:1–3)

For the next twenty-five years, Abraham and his wife waited (sometimes not too patiently) for God to give them a son. When the baby arrived, the old couple was thrilled. Abraham loved his son, but by the time the boy was twelve, his affection apparently had grown too strong. He was more devoted to his son than to God.

The Bible doesn't tell us how many alarms the old dad heard before the one described in the Scriptures, but this one was loud and clear! Seemingly out of the blue, God said: "Take your son, your only son, whom you love—Isaac—and go to the region of Moriah. Sacrifice him there as a burnt offering on a mountain I will show you" (Genesis 22:2).

What a wake-up call! We can imagine the old man shaking his head and rubbing his eyes to make sure he wasn't having a nightmare. Surely he had misunderstood! Was God really telling him to take his beloved son Isaac to a mountain and sacrifice him in the Lord's name? God couldn't possibly want him to do that, could he?

This was Abraham's supreme test. He had been in many difficult situations. Sometimes he had risen to the test magnificently; other times he had been a coward. At the moment God told him to sacrifice Isaac, everything was up for grabs. The stakes couldn't have been higher.

Abraham and the boy journeyed to the mountain. When they arrived, Abraham prepared the altar for a sacrifice. After tying the boy to the wood, he lifted the knife over his son's chest and prepared to plunge it in. Suddenly, the angel of the Lord called out to him, "Abraham! Abraham! . . . Do not lay a hand on the boy," he said. 'Do not do anything to him. Now I know that you fear God, because you have not withheld from me your son, your only son'" (Genesis 22:11–12). God then provided a ram for Abraham to offer as a sacrifice instead.

Because of Abraham's obedience to God's call, the angel of the Lord said,

> "I swear by myself, declares the LORD, that because you have done this and have not withheld your son, your only son, I will surely bless you and make your descendants as numerous as the stars in the sky and as the sand on the seashore. Your descendants will take possession of the cities of their enemies, and through your offspring all nations on earth will be blessed, because you have obeyed me." (Genesis 22:16–18)

Bondage or Freedom?
The Choice Is Ours

When Abraham heard the wake-up call from God to sacrifice his son, he had a choice—essentially the same choice each of us has when God causes the alarm to go off. Abraham didn't reach for the snooze button. He didn't try to explain his way out of God's directions. He didn't make excuses to keep his son in the center of his affection. He didn't act like he misunderstood what God was saying. Abraham faced the hardest test a parent could face.

His situation wasn't so different from what we face in our relationships today. Every day counselors and pastors hear people insist that their beloved son, daughter, spouse, parent, or friend will "die" if they don't keep fixing their problems and rescuing them from disaster. What needs to die, however, isn't a person—it's the unhealthy relationship patterns we hold on to. That's what Abraham dealt with on the mountain that day.

When we put any person in a higher position than God, that person becomes an idol in our life. In Exodus 20:3, God speaks very clearly against the sin of idolatry: "You shall have no other gods before me." Whether we want to admit it or not, enmeshment is idolatry, and idolatry is bondage.

We'll talk more about this in the next chapter, but we make another person an idol by tying our identity to how he or she sees us or by our ability to fix or rescue them. We can also become an idol in someone else's life when we start to think, *I know best how to fix you, heal you, and make your life better.*

How foolish! No matter how deeply we love, we are finite human beings who cannot see God's perspective. To claim that we have the insight or ability to heal someone or fix their problems is trying to take God's job right out of his hands.

Such idolatry robs us of the abundant life and relationships that God desires for us.

There's no doubt that one of the hardest things in life is to watch people we care about undergo crises and experience the negative consequences of their behavior. Stepping in to fix their situation may be tempting, but we can never really succeed at rescuing or saving another person because there is only one true Savior. In fact, if we always jump in to rescue others, we could actually short-circuit God's work in their life.

The moment we choose to lay down control and ownership of our "Isaac"—our husband, wife, son, daughter, friend, or other "most valuable person"—is our turning point. Leaving that individual in God's loving and faithful hands allows God to work in the other person's life—and in our own—like never before.

Who's Your Isaac?

If you're in an enmeshed relationship, there's an Isaac you need to lay down. An idol in your heart needs some attention.

Who is your Isaac? Noted Christian psychologist Diane Langberg often says, "Whatever you can't fast from controls you." So stop and think a minute. Is it your spouse? Your child? Your friend? Your fiancé? Your mentor or hero?

Consider this as well: have you put yourself in God's place in anyone else's life?

Elisabeth Elliot has noted that what we love

> holds terrible power. . . . It can blind us, shackle us, fill us with anxiety and fear, torment our days and nights with misery, and wear us out with chasing it. . . . God has allowed in the lives of each of us some sort of loss, the withdrawal of something we valued, in order that we may learn to offer ourselves a little more willingly, to allow the touch of death on one more thing we have clutched so tightly, and thus know fullness and freedom and joy that much sooner.[1]

Sometimes, the most loving thing we can do is let go . . . or say no. Most of us won't hear the angel of the Lord speaking audibly to us like Abraham did, but we will nonetheless hear a clarion call to take stock of reality, face our pain, and make the changes that bring true love and freedom to our most valued relationships. But we will also find God just as ready to provide us with everything we need to have the victory.

Break the Silence!

In some ways, God's wake-up call is the most dreaded sound in the world. Especially since our enmeshed and unhealthy relationships tend to feel so normal and right. We simply can't imagine life any other way.

Surely God wouldn't want us to hurt anyone we love, would he? But intuitively, we know the truth. We know when our hearts have become absorbed by another person. We know when we've put somebody in the center of our lives where no one but God belongs. And we know something has to be done. We dread it, just as Abraham undoubtedly dreaded every step up the mountain, but it has to be dealt with.

We must break our silence and answer the call.

We'll be tempted to resist, because we've told ourselves that the payoff we've been living for is good enough. We'll want to resist because answering the call means facing up to the lies we have lived by and owning up to our greatest fears.

We'll resist because we'll be forced to set new goals for our relationships, and because responding to the call puts at risk everything we have believed about life and love. And we'll resist at having to let go of the false identity we have created for ourselves.

Each of these identities has a common denominator: a misunderstanding of what true love is. Each role will require its own measure of courage to move out of. But we are able because our God is able.

Do you find yourself in any of these roles?

• **Fixers** feel better about themselves when they are handling someone else's problems. They thrive on feeling indispensable, yet the underlying fear they never dare articulate is, "Who would I be if the person I love didn't have this problem?"

To leave this identity behind, fixers must learn to respect people enough to speak the truth and let them make their own choices—even if those choices are self-defeating.

• **Performers** have so successfully achieved in their chosen field that they've earned a great deal of respect and adulation—things that feed their insecurities. The applause may temporarily feel good, but still they live in continual fear of failure, convinced they're only as good as their last dance. And that's a lonely and painful place to be.

To let go of this identity, performers have to learn to love, give, and serve with no strings attached.

• **Avoiders** buy peace at the price of keeping authentic relationships at arm's length. They don't let anyone get beneath the surface to see the hurt, anger, and longing inside their hearts.

To grow beyond this identity, avoiders have to learn to do the hardest thing they've ever done: trust one person enough to take a single step toward a meaningful connection.

• **Doormats** have grown accustomed to an advanced level of "helplessness" that often elicits compassion or, at the very least, rescue. Their chief desire is to avoid rocking the boat. Though they may long for people to be kind to them, doormats gravitate toward powerful (even abusive) people who tell them what to do.

It will take great courage to break out of this mind-set, but doormats must strive to find their own identity, define their desires, and become real.

• **Adrenaline junkies** are all about the thrill, the excitement. Unfortunately, they're also the first ones to take foolish risks—all because they're trying to fill an emptiness in their hearts.

To forgo this identity, adrenaline junkies have to set aside the counterfeit coping mechanisms and begin to pursue true love so that affection, trust, and genuine connection fill their hearts.

Seek True Love—And Live!

Once Michelle entered the emotional recovery process, she thought about her relationships with her domineering mother, her irresponsible brother, and her distant father. She realized that she had misunderstood the nature of love for a long time, but finally, she was getting it right. And that was confirmed in a support group session one day, when the leader asked, "What is your goal for your healing process?"

Instantly, Michelle remarked, "I want to live in truth. That's it. I want to live in truth about myself, my past, my present, my future, my family, my career, my friends, my husband and my children, and my relationship with God." Realizing what she had just said, she laughed, "I guess that's enough, isn't it? But that's exactly what I want. I lived a lie for so many years that I want to live in truth for the rest of my life."

There's no better goal for any of us. There is a beauty in this new way of life—you feel alive and can experience intimacy with God and others like never before. Your mind is free from the pressing expectations to perform or fix or devote yourself to a false idol. You are free to love and to be loved.

So listen. If you haven't heard the wake-up call yet, you will. You can count on it.

Listen as God points out the Isaac in your life. Then wake up and be obedient and faithful to his direction. Take the necessary steps to restore God to his rightful place in your heart— and then expect a liberating shift, a ripple effect in the health of all your other relationships.

In Ephesians 5:14 we are told: "Wake up, sleeper, rise from the dead, and Christ will shine on you!" The moment you awaken to God's voice will be the moment that begins to change everything.

THINK ABOUT IT . . .

1. Name some examples of the types of wake-up calls people hear.

2. Why do we often fail to respond to them?

3. What has been your goal in your most important relationships? What would it mean for your goal to change so that it's "to live in truth"?

4. How is Abraham a good model for you as you respond to God's wake-up call about an enmeshed relationship?

5. What are the parallels between Abraham's story and what you have done or still need to do in your own journey with God?

CHAPTER 5

DISMANTLING OUR IDOLS

EVERY ONE OF US IS, EVEN FROM HIS MOTHER'S WOMB,

A MASTER CRAFTSMAN OF IDOLS.

–John Calvin

Fascinating new research that is shocking the psychological world shows that children are hardwired for intimacy with a transcendent One![1] Apparently there's something about us, from the cradle to the grave, that drives us toward relationships with God and significant others. Yet anything that has that much propensity for beauty also has great propensity for pain in our lives.

When life's not the way it's supposed to be—when our relationships aren't the way they're supposed to be—we will naturally feel an emptiness and brokenness that begs for healing. Most of us will work really hard to cover up this deep-seated vulnerability. Yet we'll often get involved in unhealthy relationships to fill that void. Or, we may turn from relationships to anything else that promises to anesthetize the pain.

Exposed, Fragile, Afraid

Jamie confessed to her support group, "I've spent my entire life trying to convince people I have it all together. Even at work, I strive to do my best—not for the good of the company or to demonstrate the abilities God has given me, but to win applause (and, to be honest, to avoid any hint of a negative evaluation). With my friends, at church, in our neighborhood, and everywhere else, I want people to think I have it all together. But my husband and children know. They've seen me at my worst, and it kills me.

"Since I've been in this group, the lights have come on. I've seen that for my whole life, even the mildest criticism and the slightest failure have crushed me like an eggshell. I'm incredibly fragile. . . . There! I've said it. It's true."

Jamie wasn't the only one in the group who felt that sense of vulnerability. They all, in one way or another, felt exposed, fragile, and afraid.

People who have suffered significant and early experiences of enmeshment or isolation are much like twelve-year-olds. We don't look like junior high school kids. We wear very different clothes, drive cars, hold jobs, and have children of our own, but emotionally, we're like the scared kid in the hall who is unsure that anyone will be his friend.

We may become skilled at impressing others, but inside, we're unsure of ourselves, afraid of being known, afraid of being alone. We're trying hard to figure out how to impress people so they'll accept us. We fear the rejection of our peers, who we believe can peer into our hearts almost supernaturally and see our fear and confusion. Like the scared kid in the hall, we haven't yet resolved the crucial question, "Who am I?"

In our struggle to fit in, we sometimes exaggerate to win approval, bully others to feel powerful, form alliances to feel strong, hide from people who might hurt us, and make a myriad of dumb choices because we aren't sure how to make life work. That behavior is entirely normal for a middle schooler who is on the verge of discovering the meaning of life and can count on the wisdom and love of good-enough parents, but it's incredibly difficult for an adult who is still trying to answer the basic question of identity.

The problem for many of us isn't that our parents left us high and dry. They were involved—too involved. One may have been distant, but the other was "in our kitchen" all day every day, smothering us with directions and corrections. Whether this overinvolvement looked kind or cruel, it loudly communicated, "You're too dumb to make your own choices. You're incompetent, and you can't make it on your own."

People who have been smothered during the formative adolescent years question their decisions as adults, crave respect, and are often fearful that they have built a house upon the sand that will come tumbling down at the slightest pressure. Worse yet, such people become "carriers" of enmeshment or isolation into their own families.

Instead of God

Since Adam and Eve chose the wrong dish on the lunch menu in the garden of Eden, people have tried to fill the sin-gouged hole in their hearts with all kinds of relationships, accomplishments, and stuff. Our souls hate a vacuum and rush to fill it. Many of us are drawn into overinvolved relationships as a result. Our insecurity, emotional vulnerability, and longing to be needed drive us to idolize another person instead of God.

The problem, of course, is that God created us so that only he could fill that void. As Augustine observed, "You have made us for yourself, O God, and our hearts are restless until they find their rest in you."[2] In a similar vein, French philosopher and physicist Blaise Pascal stated, "There is a God-shaped vacuum in the heart of every man which cannot be filled by any created thing, but only by God, the Creator, made known through Jesus."[3]

Where do we find the peace, intimacy, forgiveness, and joy our hearts long for? Only in God. How are we cured from the isolation or enmeshment of relationship troubles? Only by God. No person or thing can meet the deepest longings of our heart and soul—only God can do that. To put anything other than God in the center of our hearts is idolatry.

We may think we are obeying the command of 1 John

5:21—"Dear children, keep yourselves from idols"—because we don't have any statues in our homes, but we must realize that idols are more than the Israelites' golden calf. Anything that becomes our reason for living—our motivation for behavior, our "relational fuel"—is an idol. Notice how pastor Tim Keller defines the "counterfeit gods" we pursue instead of God:

> [An idol] is anything more important to you than God, anything that absorbs your heart and imagination more than God, anything you seek to give you what only God can give. A counterfeit god is anything so central and essential to your life that, should you lose it, your life would feel hardly worth living.
>
> An idol has such a controlling position in your heart that you can spend most of your passion and energy, your emotional and financial resources, on it without a second thought. The true god of your heart is what your thoughts effortlessly go to when there is nothing else demanding your attention.[4]

Functional Saviors

Our idols aren't just intellectual concepts. They are our hearts' desire, our greatest hope, and what we love seemingly more than anything else in the world. They demand our total devotion and we crave them above all else. It is appropriate to think of our idols as "functional saviors" because we trust in them to give us meaning and happiness in life.

For those of us who are enmeshed, the idols we set up are often people . . . a perfect spouse, model kids, and ideal friendships. Keller also identifies other possible idols, including power, approval, comfort, control, and achievement. In enmeshment, we often have a blend of several of these. For instance, many of us believe another person's happiness (which is achieved by fixing his problems and controlling his life) or approval (winning her applause) will give us ultimate meaning. Others define love as power over others; they are terribly threatened by any serious challenge, and they fiercely beat down anyone who gets in their way.

When our God-given needs aren't being satisfied in relationships, we may also turn to the idolatry of an addictive behavior or substance. In his book *Addiction and Grace*, Gerald May describes addiction as "the most powerful psychic enemy of humanity's desire for God."[5] John Eldredge similarly writes, "Whatever the object of our addiction is, it attaches itself to our intense desire for eternal and intimate communion with God and each other in the midst of Paradise."[6]

Of course, we need to be careful when we talk about idolatry. The last thing enmeshed people need is someone telling them they're committing idolatry. They feel bad enough as it is! We're not trying to heap condemnation on people who already feel oppressed by shame, but idolatry is an issue of the heart that we have to deal with in order to break free from enmeshed relationships. Repentance and change can occur only when sin is clearly identified. The sin of enmeshment is putting a person in the wrong place on the throne of our lives—the place where only God rightly resides. It was Abraham's sin in his relationship with Isaac—as we've seen, David's sin in his relationship with Bathsheba, and it's the sin of anyone in an entangled relationship.

Idols Can't Deliver

No matter how desperately we pursue them, our idols can never satisfy us. Whether we idolize a relationship, a substance, or a behavior, it imprisons us. Binds us. Robs us. It draws us in more by the day. But despite the thrill or the high, it never satisfies our soul. The same is true when we idolize people. They can never make us truly happy and never satisfy our souls.

In a heart-wrenching explanation of God's desire for us to know and follow him with all our hearts, and our rabid pursuit of substitutes, the prophet Jeremiah described God as a lover we've spurned. This isn't philosophy; it's the deepest issue of our being. Jeremiah quotes God describing how he has loved and protected his people:

> I remember the devotion of your youth,
>   how as a bride you loved me
>   and followed me through the wilderness,

through a land not sown.
Israel was holy to the LORD,
    the firstfruits of his harvest;
all who devoured her were held guilty,
    and disaster overtook them. (Jeremiah 2:1–3)

Despite all God had done for them, his people eventually grew cold and didn't return his affection. They began following worthless idols with passion and tenacity.

Jeremiah compares the people's fixation on idols with the blazing passion of sexual lust. In a tragic plea, the prophet again quotes God:

Long ago you broke off your yoke
    and tore off your bonds;
    you said, "I will not serve you!"
Indeed, on every high hill
    and under every spreading tree
    you lay down as a prostitute. (Jeremiah 2:20)

Then, to drive the point home, God compares his people's lust for idols to a she-camel and a wild donkey in heat, "running here and there . . . sniffing the wind in her craving . . . who can restrain her? Any males that pursue her need not tire themselves; at mating time they will find her" (Jeremiah 2:23–24). Most of us aren't familiar with the sexual habits of pack animals, but we get the picture. Nothing can stop them from finding a willing partner and satisfying their lustful craving!

In the same way, an enmeshed person's idolatrous pursuit is strong, fierce, and seemingly unquenchable. It's not a very flattering comparison, is it? But we will continue that pursuit until we begin to see the foolishness and destruction of our quest.

The Power of Life and Death

How important to us are our cherished but misguided desires? In a piercing insight, Pastor Mark Driscoll observes that in our own sin-sick version of reality, idols are how we define heaven and hell.[7] Our goal is to use approval, power, comfort, and control to get us out of our current hell of despair, heartbreak, and meaninglessness to the perceived heaven of perfect happiness, love, and purpose.

But idols simply can't pull this heavy load. No matter how much we trust in them and how many times we think they'll give us ultimate satisfaction, the luster of approval soon fades into the fear of rejection. Our illusion of power and control slips away when something goes wrong, and our vacations, cars, and big-screen televisions no longer thrill us after a week or so.

Just as God has the power to give life, our idols have the power to kill. Tim Keller vividly describes the damage inflicted by our craving for idols. He observes that idolatry *starves* us because it takes our focus away from God—"the fountain of living water" and "the bread of life"—and leaves us empty, confused, and desperate. Our false gods *enslave* us because they demand our energy and time. Our thoughts are consumed with getting them, protecting them, and enjoying them, but like an addiction, we develop tolerance, so we always need more. Our idols also *divide* us because we compete with each other instead of loving each other. We despise people when they have more than we do.[8]

We've met Michelle already in this book. For years, she lived to please her mother, who was preoccupied with an alcoholic husband and son. The lack of stability, love, and affirmation caused Michelle to be a very fragile girl who grew into a very fragile woman. When she had empty, unhurried moments, her mind snapped like a tight rubber band back to her mom. She wondered what her mother's mood was that day, how she was reacting to her brother's latest problem-of-the-day, and how her mother would be angry if she didn't offer to help.

But Michelle almost *always* offered to help. She daydreamed many times each day about winning her mother's love, and she beat herself to death mentally and emotionally for any failure. But in fact, it didn't take real failures to cause her to spiral into self-condemnation. All she had to do was imagine a failure and she fell into the pit of despair. She called herself all kinds of horrible names—the kind you'd hesitate to call your worst enemy.

She didn't know it, but she was suffering from idol failure. Viewed somewhat clinically and dispassionately, her idolatry was winning her mother's love—an impossible achievement. This failure drove her into the abyss.

Opening Our Hearts to the Truth

Let's face it. We are quite disinclined to think of ourselves as idolaters. But when we read about idols or hear a sermon about them, it is obvious that the subject has hit a nerve. Many of us overreact and say sarcastically, "So, I'm supposed to not care at all about my son (or daughter or spouse or parent or whoever)? Are you saying I should just forget about them and their needs? And are you saying that it's wrong to have a nice car, a home, and a vacation?"

Whoa! Back up! There's nothing inherently evil about loving people, enjoying good food, getting a promotion, or having a nice car—as long as we accept them as gifts from God. The problem comes when we put those gifts in God's place and make them our supreme value. And worse, we may not even know we've done it, as we rarely (if ever) escape our well-honed skill at self-justification.

When Michelle first heard a message about idolatry, it hit a nerve. She immediately had yet another reason to beat herself up for being "a bad Christian." But the pastor wasn't condemning people for their idols. He said he wrestled with them too. And he said that Jesus died to forgive people for looking to other things instead of him. His was a message of hope and change, not bitter blame and shame. That helped Michelle to reexamine what was taking place in her heart.

Biblical counselor and author David Powlison gives us a starting point for determining if we've set up people, things, and power as idols in our hearts:

> The issue of idolatry is the most basic question of the human heart: "Has something or someone besides Jesus the Christ taken title to your heart's functional trust, preoccupation, loyalty, service, fear and delight?" Questions . . . bring some of people's idol systems to the surface. "To who or what do you look for life-sustaining stability, security, and significance? What do you really want and expect [in life]? What would make you happy? What would make you an acceptable person? Where do you look for power and success?" These questions or similar ones tease out whether we serve God or idols, whether we look for salvation from Christ or from false saviors.[9]

In addition to asking these questions, Bishop William Temple adds that we get a clear glimpse of our hearts' real treasure when we're alone in the empty, unhurried moments of life. When we have nothing else to occupy our minds, where do our thoughts drift? Do we think about how we can fix someone's glaring problem (again)? Do we daydream about getting the love we've craved? Do we look for magazines with the latest fashions or fishing gear to take our minds off the gnawing pain we feel? Do we imagine winning the lottery and having money to burn? Or are we amazed by God's grace and thank Jesus for loving us so much even though we're so flawed?

Our emotions can also be a window into our souls. What makes us anxious? What produces outbursts of self-condemnation? What provokes our fears? What brings happiness and relief? If we take time to observe our emotions, we might see a clear pattern emerging. We need to notice not only the painful emotions but the times when our affections, hopes, and joys are kindled. If we have misunderstood the nature of love, we'll have intense feelings on both sides—pleasant and painful, hopeful and haunting—but most of our thoughts will be about the person or thing standing in the center of our heart's desire.

Breaking Free from Idolatry

"Idols cannot simply be removed. They must be replaced," Keller writes. "If you only try to uproot them, they grow back; but they can be supplanted. By what? By God Himself, of course. But by God we do not mean a general belief in His existence. Most people have that, yet their souls are riddled with idols. What we need is a living encounter with God."[10]

A living encounter with God is the key to breaking free from idolatry. An iron will or self-determination to "do better" are worthless. Apart from God, we will stay stuck in these entangled relationships. God longs for us to break free, and he will walk with us each step of the way. For Michelle, breaking free started with a choice.

Michelle knew that valuing her mother's approval above all else in life was her idol, but she didn't know what to do about it. She had asked God to take it away, but when that didn't work, she wondered if God really wanted her to be free from her sin. Later, she realized that getting rid of the idol of her mother's approval would be a lifelong struggle. In order to put God first, she would need to keep trusting him for his wisdom, forgiveness, and power for the rest of her life!

"Of all the things God has done for me," she explained later, "the change in my heart has been one of the biggest blessings. I used to spend most of the day worrying, getting enraged, or feeling sorry for myself—a great life, don't you think? But I don't do that as much any more. In my relationship with my husband, I'm learning to communicate honestly about my hopes and fears. I'm learning what love that is not demanding or controlling is—something I had never before experienced in my family relationships. I'm much more thankful and I have far more peace. Heck, I'm almost sane!"

Guilt: Catalyst for Repentance

If we understand God's love for us, we realize that guilt isn't something to be avoided at all costs. When God shines his light on the recesses of our hearts and shows us the sin of idolatry, we have an opportunity to repent and return to enjoy the abundance of his grace. In his book *Rumors of Another World*, Philip Yancey wrote, "Guilt is the early warning sign of danger, the first rumor of something wrong."[11]

The Scriptures describe two very different kinds of guilt. One is powerfully liberating and restorative; the other crushes the spirit. Paul explained the two in his second letter to the believers in Corinth.

Paul's first letter to the Corinthians had been stern and corrective. They were coming up with new and creative ways to offend God. As their shepherd, Paul warned them to turn back to Christ. Just before he wrote the second letter, he got good news from Corinth. He wrote,

> Even if I caused you sorrow by my letter, I do not regret it. Though I did regret it—I see that my letter hurt you, but only for a little while— yet now I am happy, not because you were made sorry, but because your sorrow led you to repentance. For you became sorrowful as God intended and so were not harmed in any way by us. Godly sorrow brings repentance that leads to salvation

and leaves no regret, but worldly sorrow brings death. (2 Corinthians 7:8–10)

Constructive guilt is the realization of wrong (some call it "conviction") and the understanding that all sin stems from the Fall, when Eve wanted to "be like God," call her own shots, and control her destiny. When the Holy Spirit shines his light on an action that displeases him, he usually leads us to examine our motivations and beliefs. This examination is necessary in order to repent, which means to turn away from our faulty thinking, misplaced desires, and manipulative behavior and turn toward God's open arms of forgiveness, peace, and purpose.

This turning away from sin and toward God doesn't just happen once in life. Listening to the Spirit and turning back to God's grace becomes a lifestyle—the healthiest lifestyle we can have. Martin Luther described this lifestyle in the first of the Ninety-five Theses he nailed to the church door in Wittenberg: ". . . the whole life of believers should be repentance." As we invite the Spirit in to have his way, we'll become more aware of our sinful attitudes and increasingly attuned to God's amazing love and grace.

The second kind of guilt Paul described is "worldly sorrow" that leads to "death." This kind of guilt is often called shame. Guilt is feeling bad for something we've done, but shame is feeling bad for who we are. Shame pulverizes our hearts, poisons our motivations, and drives us to cover ourselves in every way so that no one can see who we really are. That's the reason Adam and

Eve sewed fig leaves to cover themselves after they sinned. Our fig leaves are a bit more sophisticated, but they're designed to accomplish the same thing.

In response to the Spirit shining his light in the dark places in our hearts, some of us are purveyors of emotional and relational death by blaming others for everything that's wrong. Yet others wallow in self-condemnation and self-hatred because they feel so rotten. *Sure, I believe God forgives other people,* they think to themselves, *but his grace doesn't extend quite far enough to reach me.*

Instead of experiencing the cleansing and freedom of forgiveness, they do emotional penance. They come up with all kinds of seemingly selfless behaviors, from washing dishes to following a rigid schedule of Bible reading, to prove that they're good people. But no matter how much they do, it's never enough—it never truly washes them clean nor restores a love relationship with God or others. The hole in their hearts can only be restored by the life-giving grace of God.

How can you tell which kind of guilt you experience? It's pretty simple. Does your guilt lead to gratitude or self-pity? Does your response cause you to feel free or even more burdened? Do you feel like telling others about the incredible grace of God, or do you want to hide? As you learn to distinguish good guilt from bad/shaming/condemning guilt, you learn to respond to the Spirit in a way that sets you free and moves you toward even greater maturity.

Keeping God in His Rightful Place

Insecurity and idolatry aren't trivial inconveniences for people who have misunderstood the nature of love. They are at the heart of the problem. Seeing them clearly is a crucial step in finding peace and charting a course for a new lifestyle. But seeing idolatry is often hard to do.

The old maxim in psychotherapy says you can't treat what you don't see. We would add that even when you see it, it is so overwhelmingly powerful that you can't manage it by yourself. By the time many of us identify idolatry, we have developed an addictive pattern that is all-consuming, draining us of our desire for God and the ability to engage in healthy relationships. It's a quagmire of fear and anxiety, a bondage that's unrelenting. Freedom comes only when we are overwhelmed by the magnificent love of God—when we invite the living God to come alive in our hearts and surround us with his healing love.

The cure for idolatry is God's amazing grace. Our sin of putting people or things in his rightful place in our hearts necessitated the death of the Son of God. God's forgiveness humbles us—yes, we are even broken by the love that was shown on the cross. But that brokenness brings opportunity for healing and reconciliation. In the same way that the father of the prodigal son ran toward him and embraced him, our heavenly Father will run toward us, embrace us, and celebrate our return. It is for all this that Jesus willingly gave his life because he values us more than anything else in the universe.

As we embrace the truth of God's love and grace, the kindness of Jesus fills our hearts, and we put him where "that person" has been: on the throne of our lives. It doesn't mean the other person isn't important. Instead, it means that God is *supremely* important. Loving that other person well necessitates that we love God more.

Jonathan Edwards had clear insight into the problems of insecurity and idolatry. He preached passionately about the value of loving God more than anyone or anything else in the world. In *The Christian Pilgrim*, he wrote,

> The enjoyment of God is the only happiness with which our souls can be satisfied. To go to heaven, fully to enjoy God, is infinitely better than the most pleasant accommodations here. Fathers and mothers, husbands, wives or children, or the company of earthly friends, are but shadows; but God is the substance. These are but scattered beams, but God is the sun. These are but streams. But God is the ocean.[12]

THINK ABOUT IT . . .

1. Does meeting a demanding person's insistent requests bring us more security? Why or why not?

2. How would you define idolatry?

3. What does idolatry look like in the life of a person who has put someone else in the ultimate place in his heart?

4. What damage does idolatry do to us and to our relationships?

5. What is true repentance and how is it different from "doing penance"?

6. Are you convinced that God forgives you and longs for you to love him supremely? How does your attitude about him determine your view of guilt and repentance? Explain your answer.

CHAPTER 6

A NEW AFFECTION

"ONE THING I ASK FROM THE LORD,

THIS ONLY DO I SEEK:

THAT I MAY DWELL IN THE HOUSE OF THE LORD

ALL THE DAYS OF MY LIFE,

TO GAZE ON THE BEAUTY OF THE LORD

AND TO SEEK HIM IN HIS TEMPLE."

—*David, Psalm 27:4*

It is incredibly difficult to overcome a lifetime of entrenched habits, fixed and vivid memories, rigid brain patterns, manipulative feedback from a demanding person, and the adrenaline rush of pain and pleasure. Until a major crisis creates an explosive combination of desperation and true hope that shakes us to the core, we will not change. Until that crisis rocks our world, we will cling to the false hope that the person(s) with whom we share an enmeshed relationship will magically change and everybody will live happily ever after.

To be sure, there will be a few brief glimpses of change that keep our fairy-tale hopes alive, but sooner or later, a crisis illuminates the truth. We reach the dire conclusion that all our expectations are dust and ashes. We want to scream, "What have I been thinking?!" That moment, though, isn't the end of the world. It's the beginning. The beginning of hope, freedom, and a new way of living!

The Power of Our Longing

The driving hope of every human heart is to be connected to someone, to give and receive authentic love, and to feel safe and secure in a strong, sure attachment. Enmeshment is that desire on cocaine! The longing for love that we seek to fill through our enmeshed relationships isn't overcome simply by ripping ourselves away from relationships and starving our hearts. Instead, we overcome this mutual reliance by refocusing our affections and taking steps to discover what it means to truly love.

The reason we struggle so much is because at our core all people on the planet fear rejection. Our most compelling desire is to be accepted. Until we refocus our affections through the lens of true love, we will rationalize controlling and being controlled, we will justify our definition of love "because he needs me," and we will excuse people who hurt us because we're so afraid of being left alone if we speak the truth.

Trying to escape our tendency toward enmeshment by suppressing our desire for love goes against every God-given fiber of our natures. Consider Jennifer, who was caught in an abusive marriage. One night she nearly blacked out when her husband choked her. In counseling the next day, she shared what had happened, and yet wanted to rescue and protect her husband.

"We've been down this road a lot of times, and he always tells me that he's sorry," she explained. "I believe him. I'm not really worried about me. I'm worried about him." As the tears rolled down her face she continued, "I'm just so confused. I don't want to get out, but what am I going to do?"

For Jennifer, and for all of us, there's good news: God made us to be loved. We don't have to suppress that desire, and we don't have to remain stuck in relationships that are not loving. However, our longing for affection must be based on honesty, wisdom, and truth. In fact, this deep longing actually provides the impetus for a way out. "The very possibility of friendship with God," Harry King notes, "transfigures life. This tends inevitably to deepen every human friendship, to make it vastly more significant."[1]

The Affection That Captures Our Heart

Many years ago, the famous Scottish pastor Thomas Chalmers preached a sermon titled "The Expulsive Power of a New Affection." He noted that no person, power, or possession ultimately satisfies our deepest longing. Our deepest need can be met only in the person of Jesus. Instead of focusing our attention on the negative—"Just stop loving the wrong things"—he suggested that we set our hearts on "another object, even God, as more worthy of its attachment, so as that the heart shall be prevailed upon not to resign an old affection, which shall have nothing to succeed it, but to exchange an old affection for a new one."[2]

Of course that new affection must be sufficiently beautiful, powerful, and compelling to capture our hearts so that any other desire is "expelled" by comparison. *What* has the power to accomplish this feat? The amazing love, grace, and wisdom of Jesus Christ.

Wherever he went, Jesus captured the hearts of people. They responded to him with fervent fear, hatred, or adoration—but never with the bland, passive acceptance often found in modern Christianity. His claims of deity and his miracles amazed some but repelled others. His character was a dividing line to everyone he met.

Today, we're more likely to critique the sermon instead of being amazed by God's beauty and captivated by a longing to live in his presence. If we read the Bible on our own at all, we often check it off as a duty instead of devouring God's Word as the source of truth, life, and power. We may do many religious things, but our hearts may be disengaged and far from our Creator. Isaiah describes the terrible sham of *religion* as opposed to a *relationship*: "These people come near to me with their mouth and honor me with their lips, but their hearts are far from me. Their worship of me is made up only of rules taught by men" (Isaiah 29:13 NIV1984).

If Jesus is to capture our hearts, we need to know him in a new way. We need a richer, deeper grasp of the greatness of God. For me (Pat), that greater, richer, deeper knowledge came in a most unexpected way.

Rediscovering the Heart's One Delight

Years ago, I traveled to India with a group of Christians to see how God was working through a ministry there. After a couple of hours in a hot, stuffy van, on our way to a village to show the *Jesus* film, we stopped at sunset in a cloud of dust on a dirt road near a cluster of one-room houses. That road led to a honeycomb of dirt paths among the houses. The smell of curry came from every doorway. We heard the shouts of parents calling their children in for supper.

As the sun went down, we found two large trees and stretched a sheet between them as high as our ladder would reach. One of the local Christian leaders set up the projector and centered the image on the sheet. It was now pitch-black outside except for the lights coming from each open door and the flashlights around the projector. We were ready.

We went house to house to invite people to watch the film. We Americans might as well have been speaking Martian, but somehow our smiles and finger pointing communicated well enough. Almost the entire village wandered over to see this spectacle that had come to visit them.

The film began, and the image of Jesus flowed gently in the

evening breeze. I had seen this film dozens of times, but this was my first time to hear it in the Hindi language. I could almost quote the entire film in English, but this night, I didn't notice the words. As we watched Jesus move through scene after scene, I was struck by something I never noticed when I had watched the film in my native language: Jesus was smiling. He was smiling a lot!

Why was it surprising for me to notice that Jesus smiled? For the simple—and brutally honest—reason that my internal image of Jesus was quite different from the one I was now experiencing. Yes, I spoke often of the grace and love of God, but I spoke most passionately about making hard choices based on what was true and right, not about responding to Jesus with a sense of abject joy in him who delights in me. There's a difference—a big difference.

My image of Jesus was a confused blend of the macho Jesus with whip in hand cleaning out the temple, and a stiff, stained-glass Jesus holding an equally stiff, stained-glass lamb. One image is harsh and demanding; the other placid and unfeeling. That night I realized that something had to change. From that moment, I embarked on a journey to trust God to change my view of him.

I didn't go to that village with any intention that God would speak to my heart. I went so that others would hear the gospel of grace and respond. God, however, had an agenda for me that night. He wanted me to see something I'd never noticed before—something that touched me deeply and caused me to reevaluate my view of him.

As I examined the Scriptures to find more joy and gratitude, Psalm 27 spoke powerfully and poignantly to me. King David lived a passionate life during a tumultuous time in Israel's history. The heat of conflict such as David faced can either melt or mold us. It can leave us either scattered and panicked or focused and resolved. In this psalm, David mentions the temptation to fear evil men who attacked him, but goes on to say how the experience caused him to focus his attention and his heart on "one thing":

> One thing I ask of the LORD,
>   this is what I seek:
> that I may dwell in the house of the LORD
>   all the days of my life,
> to gaze upon the beauty of the LORD
>   and seek him in his temple. (Psalm 27:4 NIV1984)

This psalm forced me to ask, "Is the Lord beautiful to me? Do I delight in him?" Or do I just look to him as a Cosmic Problem Solver to get me out of trouble and make me successful? More important, do I use God to make me more effective in pleasing people and controlling them? Do I trust him enough for me to stop controlling others, let them make their own choices, and allow them to suffer their own consequences—so that they are motivated to change? I began to realize that I had to stop thinking I was called to be their savior. Instead, I had to let God be God in their life and in mine.

A New Affection for the Fearful and the Prideful

Enmeshed people who feel one-down (weak and needy) in relationships are driven by the things they dread—the fear of being abandoned, the fear of condemnation, and the fear of life spiraling out of control. They are drawn to powerful people who tell them what to do, where to go, and how to act. As they comply with the strong person's demands, they become increasingly dependent. They can't imagine living without the domination of that powerful person, and in fact, they don't want even to think about it. To them, the dominating relationship feels like love.

At some point, they experience a crisis like none they have weathered before. They realize they can't keep going in the same direction with the same expectations—but they're terrified of the prospect of change. Their minds are riveted on the relationship they've counted on for so long. They've tried to pull away before, but without the expulsive power of a new affection to fill the gaping hole, their desperation soon waned, and they passively accepted the current reality . . . again.

When they gain the power of a new affection, they have confidence that someone else loves them so much that they won't be alone. They finally grasp a faint flicker of hope for a new, strong, vibrant life of freedom, real affection, truth, trust, and joy. They have a new motivation to take a bold step toward real change.

Those who are one-up (rescuers or controllers) in the dance of enmeshment have deeply resented anyone who tried to correct them in the past. They are convinced that they're selflessly serving the needy, pitiful people around them by telling them how to live. They point to their tireless efforts and the countless resources they've used to help the addicted, the sick, the confused, and the weak. Like the elder brother in Jesus' story of the prodigal, these people feel superior to those who don't love as well as they do, who aren't as dedicated, and who don't spend as much time and resources to help others.

An air of superiority gives one-up people a strong sense of identity as rescuers. They thrive on attention and affirmation, and they get plenty of it from admirers who are amazed at all they do for others. But Jesus sees the heart. He hears the prideful sneers as one-up people talk about needy people: "I can't believe she's so incompetent." "What a loser!" "What would he do without me?" Jesus knows that such pride is often a mask for deep insecurity.

Reality comes hard for the prideful. A crisis may force them to reassess their lives and realize their thirst for control and power masks deep hurt and insecurity. When that happens, they have to choose change by releasing control and exposing their emptiness. Is it hard? More than you can imagine!

A pastor friend developed a huge ministry that eventually crumbled because of his personal insecurities. Over a cup of coffee, he shared for the first time his personal vulnerabilities in relationship to his father, who was also a national leader. He realized that at the heart of his ministry was the drive to prove that he was worthy to be his father's son.

"My dad was so busy and emotionally distant that I hardly knew him," he said. "Dad didn't even play one game of catch with me. I taught myself to shave.

"I was driven to prove that I had worth and value. I destroyed a lot of people trying to fill the emptiness in my own heart. I wasn't able to change until I realized I couldn't take responsibility for my dad's failure to love me and be there for me."

While this man medicated the emptiness by becoming a ministry workaholic, others of us anesthetize the pain by turning to drugs, alcohol, pornography, food, or shopping. Some of us just go numb inside. But those who are one-down and one-up can expel their fear and pride with the magnificent love found in the gospel of Jesus Christ. We come to him with empty hands. We have nothing with which to impress him or twist his arm to get him to love us. Instead, we stand before him completely exposed, and we find that he loves us anyway.

Our Longing Fulfilled

In the gospel of Christ, God offers the attachment for which the human heart longs: we are wonderfully made, tragically fallen, deeply loved, completely forgiven, and warmly accepted in Christ. When we accept Christ's death as the payment for our sins, we experience the joy of freedom from guilt and shame. We also enter into a rich relationship with God as his children and heirs: "The Spirit you received brought about your adoption to sonship. And by him we cry, 'Abba, Father.' The Spirit himself testifies with our spirit that we are God's children. Now if we are children, then we are heirs—heirs of God and co-heirs with Christ" (Romans 8:15–17).

God sets us free, but not adrift into confusion and isolation. He frees us from the prison of sin and shame so that we can genuinely know him, delight in him, and find more meaning than we ever imagined. When we begin to grasp this truth, it thrills our hearts. This new affection begins to crowd out the fear and arrogance that has dominated us for so long.

We become children of God at the instant we say yes to him, but the process of expelling the old dreads and delights takes time. Assisted by the determination and power of the Spirit, the anxiety, compulsive behaviors, and other feelings, thoughts, and behaviors that are part of our old way of living gradually fade away. Change doesn't happen by gritting our teeth and trying to force it. Old habits and desires are expelled by a deeper grasp of the loving attachment we have with God.

To catch a glimpse of such love changes everything. And it can happen in one unexpected moment.

Ben was a teen who struggled with his weight. Guys at school always made fun of him for being a "big fatso" and having an ice-picked face full of acne. One day, his dad saw the kids taunt him. Ben just hung his head in shame.

Ben's father reached out, slung his arms around his son, kissed his forehead and said, "I could live for another thousand years, but that would not be enough time to thank God for you. You are mine! And I am so proud to call you MY son!"

That moment was a healing one for Ben's heart. It forever changed his destiny. In that moment he experienced his father's love and caught a glimpse of his heavenly Father's awesome love for him.

Like Ben, each of us is loved by an Eternal Father who is there for us. The message of the gospel raises fearful people out of the quagmire of doubt and shame to the heights of joy. The willingness of the God of the universe to pay the ultimate price for our sins humbles prideful people. As our longing for attachment is fulfilled through our relationship with God, we "taste and see that the LORD is good" (Psalm 34:8). Like the woman who barged into a Pharisee's house to demonstrate her gratitude for Jesus' love and forgiveness (Luke 7:36–50), we can't hold back our thankfulness. He means more to us than anyone or anything! We're overwhelmed by his love for us.

Wonder, love, and delight in God's grace is the expulsive power of a new affection. We find it in the smile of Jesus. Augustine captured the wonder of Jesus when he wrote,

"Man's maker was made man that He, Ruler of the stars, might nurse at His mother's breast;

that the Bread might hunger, the Fountain thirst, the Light sleep, the Way be tired on his journey; that the Truth might be accused of false witness, the Teacher be beaten with whips, the Foundation be suspended on wood; that Strength might grow weak; that the Healer might be wounded; that Life might die."[3]

Called to a New Affection

The intensity of our delight in God is a measuring stick of our grasp of his grace, but choosing to delight in God does not necessarily mean that we don't delight as much in other things. Occasionally, these preferences come as the spontaneous overflow of our affection for Christ. At other times, these decisions come through gut-wrenching and heartbreaking trials. Our commitment to delight in the Lord, however, provides a window for us to see deeply into our own hearts. We can look through this window to ask ourselves who we love, what we value, and why we do what we do. This analysis often opens our eyes to the fears and misguided goals that cause us to be one-down and the pride that drives us to be one-up, and gives us clear direction for our choices.

For example, many of us thirst for attention. We're jealous when others are praised, and we hide our failures to protect our reputations. But the power of our affection for Christ invites us to make the opposite choice. The power of his affection for

Christ prompted Paul to look at his lofty position in Judaism (cited in Philippians 3:2–6) and conclude that it was "rubbish," or more accurately translated, "dung": worthless and detestable. To Paul, the thrill of knowing Christ easily surpassed his previously precious reputation and position.

Our joy in the Lord leads to authenticity in our relationship with him. If we genuinely enjoy him, we become more sensitive to those things that block our relationship with him. Spiritual authenticity propels us to become honest—ruthlessly honest—about the full range of human conditions. It prompts us to ask the hard questions when times are tough, not to gloss over them with simple solutions and shallow answers that lead us back to our familiar position of one-up or one-down.

Job's relationship with God was authentic enough that he was willing to query God about the tough stuff. God never gave the answers Job was looking for, but at no time did God rebuke Job for asking. Job did, however, get the answer he needed. God described his power and authority over all of nature. He said in effect, "I am the Almighty God, the sovereign Creator. That's enough of an answer for you." And it was. Job remembered what he had forgotten: God was worthy of his greatest affection.

Many times in the Gospels, Jesus called people (and by extension, us) to a complete devotion—not to a church or a set of religious behaviors, but to him. The inherent question posed to all of us is: Is Jesus worthy of my highest loyalty and deepest love? Only when the carefully considered answer is yes does our new affection for him expel anything and anyone that competes for his rightful place in our hearts.

Delighting in God's greatness and grace is a call to reframe our thinking and renew our hearts. And make no mistake, not everybody will appreciate the change. Some people will accuse, some will criticize, and our old nature—fear and pride—will threaten to derail our new direction. This singleness of purpose requires gut-wrenching honesty, a sensitive response to the Spirit of God, tenacious commitment, and patience in the process of growth. Rigorous analysis and change are not for the fainthearted, but they're full of benefits for the courageous.

In *The Call*, Os Guinness defines our spiritual calling as "the truth that God calls us to himself so decisively that everything we are, everything we do, and everything we have is invested with a special devotion and dynamism lived out as a response to his summons and service."[4]

Christ's invitation to follow him and his directive to take up our cross each day isn't about serving and giving until we're exhausted. It's about loving him with all our hearts, souls, minds, and bodies. Is he worthy of that kind of love and loyalty to you?

A Wholehearted Commitment to Change

Half-hearted measures to deal with enmeshment seldom make a dent in the problem. Incremental steps usually leave us slipping back into the same place. We won't change until and unless a new affection drives out the old ones. When we see the contrast, we become tenacious, determined, and demanding—in a good way. The problem and the solution are no longer "out there" but "in here." Instead of blaming others for our faults and heartaches, we take responsibility for our new choices.

Transformation occurs when we are no longer *trying* to break free from these relationship addictions, but are *training* to break free. Tim's and my colleague, Dr. Eric Scalise, offered the following insights on this process:

> If forsaking God is the beginning of the destructive way, then repentance—turning 180 degrees in the opposite direction—must be the first choice we make. We return to a loving Creator with humility and brokenness, and He graciously begins to restore us back to Himself. How are strongholds broken in our lives?
>
> • By having the firm foundation of Christ as Savior and Lord

- By realizing that only God in His power can remove strongholds
- By identifying strongholds by name or asking God to reveal them
- By confessing and renouncing specific sins as they relate to the stronghold area
- By thanking God for His faithfulness, His forgiveness of sin and cleansing of guilt
- By exercising God-given authority over the stronghold
- By asking God to release the person from all negative forces associated with the stronghold
- By making restitution when needed or appropriate[5]

Making these choices and seeing progress takes time. Phil, who we met in chapter 3, learned about enmeshment by reading a book, but for over a year, he didn't make any real progress in growing up emotionally. Finally, a fierce confrontation with a family member caused him to call for an appointment with a counselor. In these conversations, he realized that he had only been dabbling with change while secretly hoping that his parents, his brother, and his wife would change so he wouldn't have to. This realization put steel in his soul where there had been only putty. He would change!

He told his counselor, "Okay, I've got it now. I'm never going to give in to them again. I'm going to be strong, speak the truth, and find meaning and love somewhere else—not in another person, but in Jesus." His therapist was a bit surprised by the outburst of determination, but during the next few months, Phil took steps to make good on his promise.

He immersed himself in his church community and into the Bible to find out more about God's grace. As he became more rooted and grounded in love, he became more confident and secure in his standing with Christ. He stood up to his mother's manipulation. He told her the one word she never thought she'd hear from him: no. He felt afraid the first time he said it, but he grew a little stronger each time.

Over the course of several months, the power of a new affection transformed Phil's life. He became more self-assured and less needy and indecisive around his mother, and the chronic, mild depression that had been nagging him for years began to subside. Phil finally found a new way to live.

You can too. You were made for God and you'll never find happiness—that divine discontent will never go away, the emptiness will never be filled—until you reconnect with the One who made you. He loves you. He knows your pain. He hears your cry. When you allow yourself to grow into a new affection in your relationship with him, it will turn your life around. That's what we call a breakthrough!

THINK ABOUT IT . . .

1. How would you describe "the expulsive power of a new affection"? How does it work?

2. What are some ways pathological, enmeshed behavior is fueled by fear (in those who are one-down in relationships) and powered by pride (in those who are one-up)?

3. As you read about the grace of Christ and delighting in his love, how did you feel (thrilled, confused, resistant . . . or some other emotion)?

4. What difference would it make if you saw yourself as wonderfully made, tragically fallen, deeply loved, completely forgiven, and warmly accepted in Christ? How would it affect your sense of security and your relationship with God?

5. Which things have you cherished that pale in comparison to the matchless love and acceptance Jesus offers? How would it affect you to view Christ as having "surpassing value"?

6. To what extent have you been dabbling with change? How might the principles in this chapter propel you to think more clearly and take bold action to step out of the prison of enmeshment and into freedom in Christ?

CHAPTER 7

REFLECTIONS OF TRUTH AND LOVE

ONCE YOU LABEL ME YOU NEGATE ME . . . BUT NOW WITH
GOD'S HELP I CAN BECOME MYSELF.

— *Søren Kierkegaard*

Years before the marvels of digital photo technology, one of the biggest visual thrills for many people occurred at the annual county fair. As they walked from the tent of the bearded woman to the pie contest, they passed a set of mirrors. The first one made them look short and fat, kind of like a two-legged hippo on vacation. The second one showed them as incredibly tall and thin, and the third one distorted their shape so they looked wavy. It was a lot of fun to see themselves and their friends looking so strange. No one, though, had any illusions that they were looking at accurate reflections.

When we were children, the faces of our parents were like mirrors. If the images they reflected were accurate, they showed us what we were really like—the good, the bad, and the ugly. Good parental mirrors, though, weren't passive. They made a point of finding and reflecting the good they saw in us. Positive images are important at every stage of development, especially during the adolescent years when we intuitively ask the crucial questions that form our identity and define our purpose in life. We desperately needed consistently honest, encouraging reflections to give us confidence, affirm our strengths, and correct us without crushing us.

For many children, the reflections we saw in our parents' faces were more like the ones at the county fair—but they weren't amusing. We believed that those reflections were accurate. Scowls, grimaces, looks of disgust—or worse, indifference—shook our world and distorted our sense of identity. The faces we saw and the messages coming out of our parents' mouths communicated, "What's the matter with you?" "I can't believe you're so stupid!" "You'd better shape up, or else!" "Who wants you anyway?"

To make things more confusing, some of the reflections weren't scowling. We thought they were loving, but they felt just as devastating as the scowls. They said, "I'll do that for you because you can't do it for yourself." Those negative reflections fed our insecurities and caused us to look for something—anything—that promised to make us feel better about ourselves.

We Still Need Mirrors

Suzanne grew up believing her family was completely normal. Her father's job required him to travel four days a week, and her mother was preoccupied with her younger brother's perpetual behavioral problems—including fights, smoking weed, skipping school, constant lies, and vandalism.

Suzanne's parents were preoccupied with her brother, so she felt like an afterthought. No matter how hard she tried to win her mom's and dad's attention, they didn't seem to notice. Every conversation was about her sibling. Gradually, Suzanne developed a nagging, pervasive sense that she didn't measure up—and she strongly suspected she never would. She felt desperate and detached. By the time she got married and had teenagers of her own, she found herself trying desperately to control her daughters' behavior and attitudes. After yet another shouting match, she finally realized something was wrong— terribly wrong—but not with her girls . . . with her. Gradually, she began to understand how much her childhood had shaped her view of herself and her most important relationships.

Your past isn't the past if it is still affecting your present. Some of us are many years removed from daily interaction with our parents, but the damage remains. We need to find new mirrors to reflect truth and love into our lives. If we are to grow into our full potential, it is imperative that we find mirrors that reflect the whole truth. We don't need people to give us empty, bland affirmations. Instead, we need people to "speak the truth in love"—the truth that we're flawed, but incredibly valuable.

In the last few years, some models of public education have tried to overcome the epidemic of low self-esteem in young people by elevating grades, eliminating competition, and speaking only positive remarks to the students. The motivation may have been noble, but the attempt has largely failed because to become a fully functioning person, everyone needs both truth and love—and truth sometimes is hard to hear. We don't grow or thrive without this powerful combination.

Although he was writing about the intricate working of the body of Christ, Paul's insight into our developmental needs in relationship to other people helps us to understand the power of authentic, affirming communication that does not avoid the whole truth. He first described powerful, positive relationships, and then he wrote,

> Then we will no longer be infants, tossed back and forth by the waves, and blown here and there by every wind of teaching and by the cunning and craftiness of people in their deceitful scheming. Instead, speaking the truth in love, we will grow to become in every respect the mature body of him who is the head, that is, Christ. From him the whole body, joined and held together by every supporting ligament, grows and builds itself up

in love, as each part does its work. (Ephesians 4:14–16)

Sadly, many of us are like infants—self-absorbed and demanding. Instead, we need to invite the powerful blend of God's Word, God's Spirit, and God's people to speak truth into our lives and radically transform us from the inside out.

We Need the Mirrors of God's Eyes and His Word

Where can we find reflections of the truth that will help make us whole?

The Bible teaches that we were created in the image of God. The best place to start is to look into the mirror of God's eyes. While that image is tarnished by sin and brokenness, in the eyes of the God of the universe, every person is of inestimable value. The psalmist wrote:

> When I consider your heavens,
>   the work of your fingers,
> the moon and the stars,
>   which you have set in place,
> what is mankind that you are mindful of them,
>   human beings that you care for them?
> You have made them a little lower than the angels

and crowned them with glory and honor.
You made them rulers over the works
of your hands;
you put everything under their feet. (Psalm
8:3–6)

Each one of us is unique. Loved. Thought of. Cared for. God is mindful of us, and he crowns us with glory and honor.

C. S. Lewis understood the truth of who we are before God. He used fanciful children's stories to reflect back to us powerful spiritual truth. In *Prince Caspian*, Aslan, the Christ-figure in the stories, told the children what it means to be fully human: "You come from the Lord Adam and the Lady Eve. And that is both honor enough to erect the head of the poorest beggar, and shame enough to bow the shoulders of the greatest emperor on earth; be content."[1]

We are God's dearly loved children, and he has given us a powerful sense of purpose. Throughout the Scriptures, God loudly and boldly speaks truth and love. His grace humbles our pride and dissolves our shame. As we experience his affection, we grow up to honor the family name and enter the family business of changing the world. As the ultimate loving parent, our heavenly Father sometimes takes us through tough times of training, and he disciplines us to get us back in line when we've veered off course.

The Bible offers a wealth of truth about every aspect of life: our identity, God's purposes, the nature of grace, the definition of love, resolving conflict in relationships, and all the other things that really matter. Yes, they were written thousands of years ago in another culture, so it takes some digging to uncover the treasure buried there, but it's worth it.

When Suzanne faced the painful truth about her strained relationship with her daughters, she felt confused. She had been faithful to go to church her whole life. What happened? How could her relationship with her kids and her husband be so painful? She found a Christian counselor who explained that God wants us to experience his truth "in the innermost places." Throughout her life she had avoided looking deep into her heart. Now, when she looked, the darkness almost swallowed her. But the counselor told Suzanne that God meets her even in the darkest places. In the weeks of counseling, she also found a small group that is committed to applying God's truth to life's deepest disappointments. The counselor and new friends became new mirrors reflecting truth and grace. Slowly, Suzanne's perception of God, herself, and her family began to change.

If you don't have a friend, pastor, counselor, or group like Suzanne found, look for one. And don't quit until you find one!

Be sure as well to use a version of the Bible that's easy to read. We would like to recommend the *Bible for Hope*, edited by Dr. Tim Clinton, which contains 116 life topics as a helpful resource. Find one that gives insights about the passage you're reading, and dive in. Don't be discouraged if you don't understand. Talk to your friend, a pastor, or a Bible study leader to get to the truth. You'll discover some amazing things, you'll be awed at the greatness of God, and you'll find out that you are the apple of God's eye.

Author and spiritual leader Thomas Merton was an avid student, and he loved God's Word. He wrote, "By reading the Scriptures I am so renewed that all nature seems renewed around me and with me. The sky seems to be a pure, cooler blue, the trees a deeper green. The whole world is charged with the glory of God and I feel fire and music under my feet."[2]

We Need Mirrors of Flesh and Blood

In Western culture, and especially in the rugged individualism of America, we often think of Christianity as a solitary event instead of a team sport. As we see in Paul's letter to the Ephesians, his other letters, and throughout the Bible, we need others to help us grow strong in our faith and develop our identities as believers. Some of us regularly read the Bible about the character of God and our identities as his children, but strangely, it doesn't make much of a dent. Reading is only part of the equation; we need the flesh-and-blood mirrors of other people to reflect the truth God wants to impart to us. Proverbs reminds us, "As iron sharpens iron, so one person sharpens another" (Proverbs 27:17).

Truth and grace come from God's Word, in relationship with God's people, and by the working of God's Spirit in our hearts. We can't leave out any of these and make real progress.

In Hebrews 10:24–25, Paul challenges us: "And let us consider how we may spur one another on toward love and good deeds, not giving up meeting together, as some are in the habit of doing, but encouraging one another."

In our confusion about the nature of love, we made a host of mistakes in relationships. We felt insecure, so we looked for people who would smother us with love instead of treating us with respect. Or we were threatened by our fears, so we compensated by dominating those around us. And we returned the favor, smothering some, dominating others, ignoring some who needed us, and trying to fix people instead of loving them enough to let them learn from the consequences of their choices.

In all these behaviors, we hoped people would praise us for being "loving," "good leaders," "self-sacrificing," and other accolades. That's the reflection we wanted to see in the mirror. We got enough praise to keep us going, but these affirmations were only part of the truth. These reflections perpetuated our pathology rather than being a catalyst for change.

Now, we realize we need a different set of mirrors. We need people who are secure—who aren't dependent on us or intimidated by us. True friends. As Proverbs 27:6 puts it, "Wounds from a friend can be trusted, but an enemy multiplies kisses." We need friends who affirm and speak the truth. We need friends who won't walk away when we have a hard time "getting it." Our friend Phil found a friend like that.

Thomas had been around the block a couple of times in

dealing with his own problems defining love. When Phil met him, they became fast friends. After a few months, they trusted each other enough to be open and vulnerable. They had rich conversations—the kind that went far below superficial talks they'd had with "friends" their whole lives.

One day, as Phil shared some of the shame he felt because he could never measure up to others' expectations, Thomas asked, "When you think about all this when you're alone, what do you call yourself?"

Phil's expression showed that he didn't quite understand, so Thomas asked it another way, "When you're at your worst, what names do you call yourself?"

Phil looked like he had just dropped his pants in public. He felt exposed by his friend, but he knew he was safe enough to tell the truth. Under his breath, he mumbled a long line of foul, curse-laden epithets—names he called himself without even thinking about them.

Thomas asked, "Who else would you call those names?"

Phil's eyes widened, "Only my worst enemy."

"Precisely," Thomas said.

That moment was a turning point for Phil. He realized his self-loathing and shame was continually wrecking his heart. Since childhood, when he instinctively asked, "Who am I?" the horrific, soul-pulverizing answer came from his own mind and his own lips. Now, his new insight gave him a point of repentance, and he began to make some changes in his thinking.

Suddenly, all the truths about his identity in Christ sent

down deeper roots. He had known those things before, but his shame had formed a barrier that couldn't be bridged—until a friend had the perception, experience, and compassion to be a good mirror and speak the truth in love.

Act on What You See

It's not enough to just gaze into mirrors and enjoy the view, or to turn away from what we don't want to see. Mirrors help us know how to act. In fact, James used the analogy of a mirror to communicate the importance of acting on what we see in God's Word. He wrote,

> Do not merely listen to the word, and so deceive yourselves. Do what it says. Anyone who listens to the word but docs not do what it says is like someone who looks at his face in a mirror and, after looking at himself, goes away and immediately forgets what he looks like. But whoever looks intently into the perfect law that gives freedom, and continues in it—not forgetting what they have heard, but doing it—they will be blessed in what they do. (James 1:22–25)

People who see themselves as victims tend to be passive, waiting for someone to make things right for them. That strategy, however, doesn't work for spiritual and relational growth. In fact, James calls it deceit. *Ouch!* James encourages us to get up, take action, speak truth, and make new, bold choices with growing confidence in God.

As we read the Bible and talk to our friends, we see points where we need to change: to speak up or shut up, to take the initiative to care for someone or to stop helping those who need to make their own choices, to quit smothering and give people room to breathe, and to stop dominating and let people make their own choices without fear of condemnation. In all these choices (there are many each day), we need the feedback, affirmation, and correction of friends who love us enough to speak the truth even when we don't want to hear it.

Relationships of Truth and Grace

Fear. Confusion. Insecurity. A lifetime of these patterns are huge barriers to change. Breaking through can often seem as elusive as a moving target. But the Bible offers encouragement for relationships filled with truth and grace. Important passages tell us to "love one another," "encourage one another," "admonish one another," "forgive one another," "speak truth to one another," and "accept one another." We need friends like this if we are to climb out of the quagmire of enmeshment and isolation. As valuable as these relationships are, they aren't without challenges.

Some of us stick our toe into the waters of vulnerability and true friendship, but we feel uncomfortable with the truth that's uncovered. It's easier to go back to business as usual. When a trusted friend asks if we have time to get together, we complain, "No, I'm really busy these days. Maybe some other time." Of course, a real friend sees right through us and hears, "I'm too afraid to go any deeper, so I'm using busyness as an excuse to avoid you like the plague!"

It's a fight to stay connected with a friend who understands. To remain on task and keep pushing when times get hard. From time to time, we'll want to bail out on the whole thing, but if we overcome our excuses and stay connected, amazing changes can happen.

We will need time by ourselves to think and reflect, and we will need time with friends to debrief and recharge. Jesus regularly went on retreats with his followers. If he needed to refill his tanks with love, rest, and understanding, so do we.

Our shame and pain make us pitiful or angry—or both—so we desperately grasp for people or push them away. The Bible, though, invites us to take a risk to form intimate, supportive relationships with people who understand. Not everyone will. If you're having a hard time finding quality friendships, don't stop looking, but ask the hard questions: Am I so needy that I'm running people off? Or am I so angry that no one wants to get near me? Sometimes a dose of humility is the starting point for a good friendship.

The proverb says, "As iron sharpens iron, so one person sharpens another" (Proverbs 27:17). Don't be surprised when sparks fly as you get closer to true friends. Great relationships aren't based on the absence of conflict, but the healthy resolution of it. And you'll be able to use the lessons you learn in your connections with your friends when you face the harder task of confronting the people who have hurt you.

John Bunyan, who wrote *Pilgrim's Progress*, understood the power of honest, affirming relationships: "Christians are like the flowers in a garden, that have each of them the dew of Heaven, which, being shaken with the wind, they let fall at each other's roots, whereby they are jointly nourished, and become nourishers of each other."[3]

If you've found friends like this, hug them and thank God for surrounding you with them. If you haven't yet located them, keep looking. They're out there waiting for you. Your new, stronger identity depends on it.

THINK ABOUT IT . . .

1. What did your family's mirrors reflect back to you when you were a child, especially when you were a teenager? How did those visual and verbal messages affect you for good or ill?

2. Why is it important to find a friend or two who speak both truth and love to us? What happens if one of the two is missing?

3. What passages of Scripture are the most affirming to you? Which ones challenge and correct you?

4. Have you found a friend you can trust—with whom you feel safe enough to be open and vulnerable, but who doesn't feel compelled to fix you? If you have, how has that relationship produced sparks? How has it shaped your life? If you haven't found someone like that, where can you look?

5. Why are new mirrors so important in helping us shape a new, healthy sense of identity?

CHAPTER 8

LEARNING TO LOVE WELL

LET US NOT LOVE WITH WORDS OR TONGUE BUT
WITH ACTIONS AND IN TRUTH. THIS THEN IS HOW
WE . . . SET OUR HEARTS AT REST IN HIS PRESENCE.

—1 John 3:19–20

Living our best life is about learning to love well. We may blame our past, our parents, or our ex, but the key to our future lies with us, not them.

The sad truth is, many of us are still doing relationships like when we were teenagers. You may have incredible fashion sense, amazing skills that landed you a great career, be able to keep an entire household functioning smoothly—and still have neglected your emotional growth and maturity. Minus this important element of who we are meant to be, we're prone to view ourselves as one-up or one-down—powerful and manipulative, or weak and submissive—and fluctuate between the extremes: One moment we'll control and use others to get what we want. Then we'll turn around and rescue those we care about from the consequences of their choices. We make people our "project" while we neglect ourselves. We don't set boundaries. We deny our own feelings or desires and get lost in a spiral of insecurity, self-doubt, and fear.

If any of this describes you, just keep in mind that God longs for us to experience the very best kind of love, joy, and intimacy that we can. In fact, relationships were his idea!

So how do we experience healthy, thriving relationships? We start by recognizing that we have a choice to grow up emotionally and develop healthy patterns.

Dr. Sandra Wilson has a theory that says change happens when we consistently make and practice new choices. As an adult, you have a choice in every relationship. You no longer have to live as a victim of other people's behavior and mistakes, as you may have had to as a child. You do not have to be preoccupied with keeping others happy. You do not have to keep rescuing people. You can be free to love genuinely. To set boundaries. To express your feelings honestly. You can learn to love deeply from the heart and experience safe, satisfying, stable relationships.

It all starts with the decision to be honest with ourselves and pursue a new path.

Relearning How to Love:
Three Key Choices

Breaking free from the crazy-making of relationships doesn't happen overnight. It begins when we identify our tendency to rescue, fix, or control others—and then choose an alternate response. Over time, we can give up our harmful habits and develop new, healthier ways of relating. Over time, we can learn to redefine love, trust, and responsibility.

Each of us holds to core relational beliefs about ourselves and other people. Every day we ask and answer key questions about them and us. When we have a secure relationship style, we understand that we are worthy and capable of love, and that others are willing and able to love us. This understanding opens the door to greater confidence and competence in our most important relationships in the following key areas. We'll introduce each idea here, and then discuss it more in-depth in the following chapters.

A Secure, Established Identity

Your identity is much more than your Social Security number. People cannot steal your true identity, but you can lose sight of it if you're not careful. Especially when you're dealing with difficult people.

In a nutshell, your identity is a sense of self that defines who you are and aren't, what you enjoy and what you don't, what you do well and what you can't stand. Your identity includes little things like the the music you listen to and how you spend your free time. But it doesn't stop there. Your identity also includes your values and priorities, thoughts, emotions, and opinions.

Clearly, identity is shaped by the influence of friends and family, feedback from authority figures, and especially what we gather about ourselves during times of failure and pain. For example, in order to develop a healthy sense of self, children need to hear their parents communicate, "I love you. I'm proud of you. And you're really good at _____." The lack of such messages can cause some of our deepest and most damaging wounds. But to hear those things from others, especially when we're feeling low or coming off of a disappointment, goes a long way toward building a positive identity.

At the same time, we also need to develop a sense of ourselves apart from others, and especially our parents. This process is a critical task of adolescence, as we've mentioned, but many of us who grew up in overly dependent families never had this opportunity. Our parents either micromanaged and controlled every aspect of our lives, or pressured us to pick up the slack for another family member's poor choices and hold together the family image. As a result, we became either passive or controlling, defining ourselves by what we do and what others think of us. But moving toward health and sanity requires discovering who we are apart from those relational roles.

Research indicates that probably the majority of us need to embark on this journey of developing a new identity to some degree. So don't think you're the only one! And don't hesitate to seek out professional counselors, support groups, pastors, or friends who can provide the safe, loving environment you need. We can experience great healing through these relationships. They also give us opportunities to practice what we're learning about giving and receiving respect, valuing thoughts and emotions, and speaking the truth in love.

As we move toward healthier relationships, we'll find ourselves developing a more secure relational style—learning how to identify and communicate thoughts, feelings, and opinions with confidence.

Wise Trust

Because you are reading this book, Pat and I (Tim) are assuming that you either trust too much or too little. Some of us hold to an immature trust that lets people be privy to things we shouldn't tell them—exposing ourselves to hurt, ridicule, and betrayal—or that causes us to let down our guard to people who have hurt us and are not sorry.

Especially when it's someone we have a long history with, we may hope that trusting them again will somehow cause them to feel sorry for us—or maybe give us a little leverage, a bargaining chip. We don't realize that manipulative people lick their chops at a naïve person who blindly trusts them.

Jan is a great example—a well-meaning but gullible woman who refuses to break up with her boyfriend even though he is cheating on her and is verbally and physically abusive. In her mind, he's "really a nice person," simply because he's stuck around. But the rest of us clearly see her bruises and his manipulation.

Rob's story is along the same vein—he works overtime, often late into the night, to pick up the slack for his coworker. Why? "He told me our boss is slamming him with work right now, and I don't want him to lose his job." That's how Rob sees it, but the reality is that Rob's coworker is out drinking away the pain of his recent divorce.

By his misplaced trust, Rob enables his colleague's irresponsibility. By her blind trust, Jan feeds her boyfriend's abuse. When we trust without reason, we are setting ourselves up to get hurt and be taken advantage of.

On the other end of the trust continuum, some of us have been burned and are determined not to let it happen again. We've withdrawn to protect ourselves from risk, and we refuse to engage with anyone—even those who genuinely love us—in a meaningful way. We live by the mantra: "Hurt me once, shame on you. Hurt me twice, shame on me."

Becky lives this. The model employee, a committed wife, and a great mom, she'd do anything for you, but she never allows anyone to get too close. Give Becky any project or task, and she'll move heaven and earth to get it done. But if you ask her how she's *really* doing—if you try to have a meaningful conversation with her and really engage her heart—she'll likely respond with a surface answer and move on to another topic.

Becky can't let anyone in. She is overwhelmed with anxiety and fear that other people will just use her and then cast her aside. She's not able to relax in the fact that others genuinely love and care for her.

When we live on the extremes of trust, we're unable to accurately appraise a relationship and its potential for harm or good in our lives. Wise trust is grounded in relational evidence developed over time. Simply put, "It's a general belief that others . . . are capable and willing to meet [our] emotional needs."[1] When we trust someone, we're in essence saying, "I can rely on you. I know you will be honest with me, and I am confident that despite the fights and storms we have, you will care for me, value me, and not intentionally hurt me."

In the context of a safe relationship, trust opens the door to intimacy, vulnerability, and emotional connectedness. But we don't make ourselves vulnerable with just anyone. The farther we get from our unhealthy attachments, the better we're able to discern who to draw close to and who should arouse suspicion. The victim or the rescuer role is no longer ours. We understand that trust is precious, and it must be earned. So when we interact with someone who is abusive, controlling, or emotionally absent, the "trust alarm" goes off, reminding us to create some space—set appropriate boundaries—to protect ourselves.

Our faith also grows as we release the most important

people in our lives to God. Rather than taking things into our own hands—trying to control and manipulate them to feel secure—we remember that God is actively involved in our relationships, and he can be trusted to work for our good.

Here's a final introductory thought about trust. Even as we seek to change, we must be careful where we place our faith. Our history has been to trust in ourselves or other people. When we forget that the center of our faith and affections is Jesus alone, we will be like Peter walking on the water: "But when he saw the wind, he was afraid and, beginning to sink, cried out, 'Lord, save me!'" (Matthew 14:30).

The relational storm in our lives may be a parent, a spouse, a friend, a boss, a brother or sister, or even a child who is somehow causing fear in our hearts: Fear of losing them. Fear of their anger. Fear of rejection. If we focus on them, we'll lose sight of Jesus, our Peace. But if we cry out, "Lord, save me!"—if we invite him into our struggle and ask him for wisdom and strength—we can move from fear to faith, because "perfect love casts out fear" (1 John 4:18 NIV1984).

While no one except Jesus will ever love us perfectly, building our life on this truth enables us to identify and move away from any relationship that is bound up in fear. We can then invest ourselves in people who are authentic and safe rather than manipulating or controlling. And out of this newfound ability to trust wisely, we can begin to experience intimacy and emotional connectedness without fear of abandonment and take steps to protect ourselves from abusive and domineering people.

Balanced Responsibilities

If there's one thing that enmeshed people know, it's how to take responsibility! And yet, it's often a responsibility turned purely outward, toward others, rather than inward, caring for themselves.

Take Casey, for example. She wants to be a good mom, and in her mind, that often involves bailing out her daughter, Stefanie. "Stef just isn't that good at school," Casey confided in a friend one day. "If I don't write her papers for her, she'll fail . . . and I will not have my daughter dropping out of high school." Often, Casey stays up late into the night editing and rewriting her daughter's compositions. She feels drained and exhausted—emotionally and physically—but doesn't know what to do differently.

What's ironic is that while Casey is taking on too much responsibility for her daughter, she isn't taking any responsibility for her own life or health. An enmeshed person, in essence, says, "My problems, needs, and desires aren't important. I exist to take care of *your* problems, meet *your* needs, and make *you* happy."

Learning to take appropriate responsibility means putting yourself back in the driver's seat of your life rather than being controlled by the demands of others. It means determining what is and isn't your burden to bear, and then setting corresponding boundaries.

While we are called to help and encourage each other (Galatians 6:2), each one of us is responsible to the Lord for our particular load—not anyone else's. Galatians 6:5 says, "For each will have to bear his own load" (ESV). That means we can't shift the blame for neglecting our own well-being to our parents, spouse, boss, or kids.

Change in this area begins with stepping back and taking stock of our lives. Are you assuming someone else's responsibility at your expense? Are you playing the victim and blaming someone else for your choices?

When Michelle, who has so honestly shared her story with us, reflected on her relationship with her alcoholic father, her irresponsible brother, and her domineering mother, she told her counselor, "You talk about being stuck in adolescence, but I was more like a five-year-old! My identity was set in concrete. Wow, was it twisted! I was only what my mother wanted me to be. I idolized her and tried to shape myself into her image. Crazy, I know. She had me thinking I was responsible for everything. If anything went wrong, I was sure it was because I failed to prevent it in some way or another. I wasn't just overly attached to her; I was completely absorbed!"

Through her support group, Michelle found a mentor who gave honest feedback and helped her learn new priorities. She began to take responsibility for her own choices. She learned to be assertive without being driven, and to be helpful without being addicted to the relationship. And she learned to set boundaries.

In their book *The Flight from Intimacy*, Janae and Barry Weinhold explain that boundaries provide a structure to keep people from crossing into each other's space.[2] Like neighborhood fences, they help identify what is "yours" and what is "mine." Poet Robert Frost once wrote, "Good fences make good neighbors."[3] Appropriate boundaries allow you to be separate from others physically, mentally, emotionally, and spiritually, and to create safety in relationships.

There is a fine line here. Tim and I (Pat) are not encouraging you to just throw up your hands, walk out, and cut yourself off from everyone around you. Our desire is to help you gain a balanced understanding of love that allows you to help bear another person's burdens without overextending yourself. To accurately assess the situation, your emotional investment, and the risks at hand, and ask yourself: *Where do I give in and where do I push back? What is appropriate? Just? Loving? Gracious? Kind? Sincere? And necessary . . . right now and in the future?*

Psychologists Henry Cloud and John Townsend—experts on this topic—say that when we clearly know what to take responsibility for—what we need to own and what we don't—it frees us.[4] How can this be? Aren't boundaries limits? How, then, can boundaries *free* us?

For one, healthy boundaries serve to keep the good in and the bad out. They allow us to enjoy and experience close relationships like never before—protecting us from harm but also offering safety to the other person.

Often, the first step in setting a boundary is the hardest one: saying no. For many of us, we fear that if we don't take responsibility for the consequences of those we love, everything will fall part. Think of the guy who threatens his girlfriend, "If you break up with me, I'll kill myself." Or the twenty-something who tells his parents, "If you don't let me live here, I'll end up a homeless drug addict." In such situations, the very idea of setting boundaries with people is terrifying. No one wants to carry the guilt of wondering, *What if I had done more?*

To a hyper-responsible person, this is an emotional quandary of the worst kind. *After all,* they reason, *God has rescued me. Had it not been for his mercy, goodness, and grace, where would I be?* But as we look more closely at the nature of God, we see definite boundaries. If God wasn't both loving and just, he would never draw a line in the sand and allow people to spend eternity in hell. Scripture imposes clear consequences for repeated rejection of God's grace and love. Even as we strive to give, serve, and love like Jesus, we discover that we must learn to love with limits.

As "fixers" and enablers, we can rationalize any action we take. But the moment we decide, "I'm not going to put up with this anymore" and set a boundary, then everything changes— as Michelle was finding out.

One night, she reported to the group, "I've made a lot of progress lately. I'm up to junior high!" People laughed, but they knew this was a remarkable improvement. Michelle later told them, "I'm having to sort out a lot of messes in my life. I've taken responsibility for everybody's well-being but my own. Now I realize not all my 'helping and loving' has been for their sake at all. In a sense, I see how my actions gave me value and a certain power to get people to appreciate me. Wow, this is a whole new world!"

The process of healing is a journey. Many times, doing the right thing will feel strange and even wrong. You're sure to feel some false guilt along the way too. That's why it's so important to have someone you can trust to help you see the world through a clearer lens, ensuring that you take responsibility for you and you alone.

The Journey toward
Loving One Another

Perhaps you can identify with the people in this chapter. Whether you're Jan, Rob, Becky, Casey, or Michelle, the good news is, you can do this! The four areas we've discussed have amazing potential to help you break free from whoever and whatever has a hold on you so you can begin to develop new relationship skills.

The journey of breaking free and moving into safe, loving relationships takes time, determination, and a whole lot of God's grace. It's like learning to ride a bike all over again, only this time out of a sincere heart rather than out of fear.

For Casey, change might start with telling her daughter, "I

love you, honey, but I cannot continue to rescue you from your procrastination. Your grades are your responsibility, and my responsibility is to be your mom."

For Jan, healing might start with telling her abusive boyfriend, "I will not let you continue to treat me this way. You can say whatever you want, but it's not love. I deserve to be cherished, pursued, and honored by the man I marry."

For Rob, breaking free might begin with setting some clear boundaries, like telling his coworker, "I care about you, man, but I can't keep covering for you. It's draining me and taking me away from my family. Your work is your responsibility. I'll be your friend, but I can't rescue you."

Let me (Pat) warn you, things often get worse before they get better. Because emotional and relational wounds go deep, any time we try to bring change, we can expect to hit walls of disappointment that make us want to give up. "It's just too much to face," our buddy Phil told one of his friends. "When I started down this road, I thought I'd feel a lot better about things in a month or so. This is brutal!"

Phil's friend helped him understand that the process of "growing up" in relationships is long and complicated, just like adolescence. The friend asked him to talk about what it was like when he was in junior high and high school, and they laughed at some of the dumb things Phil had done.

"So, you're saying I've got to go through a time like that again," Phil acknowledged aloud, "but this time to grow up in how I handle relationships."

His friend nodded.

"Okay, I get it," Phil smiled.

Genuine love won't feel natural at first. In fact, you might wrestle with tremendous guilt and confusion as you begin to untie the knots of enmeshment. As you change—taking appropriate responsibility; learning to set boundaries, say no, and trust wisely—you'll get a reaction from those you've been rescuing and controlling. After all, dysfunctional people have a vested interest in you staying just as you are: They want you to continue to rescue them from the consequences of their poor decisions. They don't want you to be mature and strong because it turns their world upside-down.

They'll likely accuse you of being selfish, heartless, and even cruel. They may shame you, threaten you, or bribe you to draw you back in. Will you give in to their demands and pressure? You may be tempted to. But the more you are rooted and grounded in God's unfailing love for you, and the more you're committed to doing what is best, the easier it will be to grow into a person who knows how to do relationships well.

THINK ABOUT IT . . .

1. In what ways have enmeshed people lost the power to choose, and how is this like being relationally "stuck" in adolescence?

2. Why is it foolish to give in to an abuser, trust a liar, and be emotionally vulnerable to someone who has a compulsion to control you? What kind of damage does it do to you and your relationship with that person?

3. How do you think setting appropriate boundaries and taking appropriate responsibility help us to love more sincerely?

4. What do you feel are the most difficult or painful risks we face when we seek to make changes and "grow up" in our most important relationships?

5. What relationship changes do you most look forward to as you anticipate becoming a person who can do relationships well?

CHAPTER 9

GAINING A SECURE IDENTITY

I'D LIKE TO RUN AWAY FROM YOU,
BUT IF I WERE TO LEAVE YOU . . .
I WOULD DIE.

*—Lyrics from "I Hate You, Then I Love You"
as sung by Celine Dion*

A few months after her divorce, Maria poured out her heart to her support group. "How did this happen? I gave everything I had to him, but now my life is a wreck. The more I gave, the more he demanded, and the less he gave back. I wish I could understand how it came to this point. My relationship with John has been, to be honest, a lot like my relationship with my father when I was growing up."

At the time, Maria didn't realize how true her assessment was. Our early years deeply affect our core relational beliefs—how well we do (or don't) experience intimacy and develop healthy adult relationships. Family beliefs and patterns tend to reproduce themselves across generations. For Maria, the seeds of brokenness and unhealthy behaviors were clearly related to her early family relationships.

The Gateway to Adulthood

The apostle Paul got it right when he reminded us, "When I was a child, I spoke like a child, I thought like a child, I reasoned like a child. When I became a man, I gave up childish ways" (1 Corinthians 13:11 ESV). Maturity is indeed the goal, and adolescence—that pivotal period in a person's life that so significantly shapes everything that happens for the rest of one's life—is supposed to be its access point.

What were your formative years like? Ideally, from about age twelve to eighteen, you were defining and clarifying your sense of identity and successfully integrating all you had learned about trust, self-confidence, and competence on your way to answering the question of "Who am I?" Children who accomplish this feat during the adolescent years are ready for the challenges of adulthood. In other words, they are armed with a strong sense of self, the wisdom to know who to trust, and a clear grasp of their responsibilities. Without such a stable foundation, we are more prone to act impulsively or be indecisive in relationships and major decisions as adults. We're also more likely to wither under self-doubt and shame, or be driven to control everyone and everything around us.

Your parents are crucial in this transitional process.

Although some parents believe that peer relationships are the most influential, recent studies show that the impact of parents remains primary, even as children gradually gain independence.[1] So adolescents need an attentive and attuned home environment in which they can mature into healthy, competent, confident young adults. That environment is established by parents who give children "roots and wings"— a strong foundation of unconditional love and support, along with the confidence and skills to make it on their own.

Then and Now

Do you remember how you felt back then—in junior high and high school? You tended to be:

- worried about what others thought of you
- very sensitive to criticism
- desperate to belong to a respected group
- dependent on your parents for transportation, finances, and other physical needs
- sometimes foolish about your choice of friends
- susceptible to peer pressure and false promises
- unclear about your strengths and abilities, and
- wishy-washy about taking responsibility

No wonder parenting during the adolescent stage of a child's development is both art and science! Teenagers need parents who teach clear principles about, and carefully give increased responsibility for, decision-making. Good parents will learn to stand back and let their children succeed or fail, but also remain close enough to provide affirmation, support, and honest feedback.

The goal of parents during this crucial phase is "to work themselves out of a job" as they facilitate the transformation of a young person from a self-absorbed, immature twelve-year-old to a strong, stable, confident, and competent young adult. It is an amazing process that will certainly have its ups and downs and awkward moments, but it doesn't have to be a disaster. The secret is to not only learn good parenting principles, but to become proficient in the art of knowing the proper timing and expression of those principles so that you know when to give in and how to push back.

This chapter will concentrate mostly on how our past with our parents affects us today, but if you want more on parenting your own children, make sure you read the appendix that starts on page 267.

Our Parents and Us

By the time a young person leaves home, he needs to feel secure about himself. He needs to be skilled in making all of his own choices and in experiencing the benefits and consequences of those choices. At the same time, effective parenting includes a robust focus on safety, love, and limits.

Balancing those factors is a challenge. If your parents were uninvolved and permissive, you didn't have the guidance to develop a framework of wisdom, and you probably made your share of foolish and destructive choices (unless "surrogate influences" such as grandparents, mentors, teachers, or coaches served as resources for you). Conversely, if your parents smothered you with directions until you walked out the door, you likely lacked confidence and some of the skills you needed for adulthood.

When taken to an extreme, children of parents who were overprotected, overindulged, or overcontrolled tend to demonstrate the following:[2]

OVERPROTECTING	OVERINDULGING	OVERCONTROLLING
• Lack discipline	• Tend to be selfish	• Have trouble relaxing
• Become underachievers • Become dependent	• Little sense of accomplishment • Lacks self-control	• Problems with intimacy & relationships • Passive-aggressive
• Trouble regulating emotions • Immature	• Sense of entitlement • Lack empathy, respect, tolerance for others	• Blame selves for everything • Worry too much about what others think

Parenting That Yields Shallow Roots and Clipped Wings

In disrupted families, adolescents don't develop adequate roots and wings. Perhaps your parents were so preoccupied with their own relational, financial, legal, physical, or emotional problems that they were unavailable to you—this produces withered roots. Or they may have been overly involved in your life, hovering over you, telling you what to do every moment of every day, and expecting complete compliance—this results in clipped wings. In some families, both errors are present: one parent is physically or emotionally absent and the other over-compensates by smothering the children.

Certainly, no parent is perfect. We're not suggesting that perfection is necessary anyway. Children just need "good enough" moms and dads, according to family therapist Virginia Satir. But even that is a tall order. No wonder Dr. James Dobson titled one of his books, *Parenting Isn't for Cowards!*

It takes work to have a significant influence in our kids' lives. Kids need heavy doses of time with parents who are emotionally connected to them. The problem is, the preoccupied parent misses out on many of these opportunities. However, if adolescents get enough attention, feedback, and affection, and if they get enough opportunity to try things on their own, the vast majority of them will make great strides toward becoming healthy, responsible adults.

In many families, children don't receive parenting with

love and logic (and you may have grown up in one). Parents may be too permissive, lacking clear expectations and consequences. They may fail to enforce the rules they establish, or they may establish rigid rules in an effort to control their children throughout adolescence. Each of these errors can stunt a child's development, which contributes to a deep sense of insecurity. Such an environment leaves children with a bone-deep existential or spiritual loneliness that is a setup for a lifetime of enmeshed relationships.

Children from these families often lack confidence and become desperate to cope with the problems they face. In their desperation, they *hide* from difficulties or risks because they don't feel able to face life's challenges. They strive to *dominate* so they never look weak or needy. They *please* people to win the approval they long to receive. Or they *withdraw* in despair because they don't think life has any hope or purpose.

A Setup for Enmeshment

When children from these families reach adulthood, they long to be close, to be connected, to be wanted—because God made us that way. Many of them will seek satisfaction for this longing in marriage. When the spouse fails to fill that longing, they will often turn to their children instead, hoping to satisfy their emotional needs through the parent/child relationship. This desire for a loving connection is most common in mothers, but dads may also seek fulfillment by becoming overly invested in the child.

No matter how innocently it begins, the yearning for connection in order to fill an empty heart eventually leads to the emotional dependence of enmeshment. It may look like love, feel like good parenting, and be praised by friends, but it becomes deeply destructive to everyone involved. A child-centered home is not a healthy home. It places expectations and demands on children that they should not and cannot meet.

Enmeshment may emerge as a problem for the overly involved, needy parent when a child is in grade school, but most often, it bursts into all its dysfunctional glory when the child becomes an adolescent. Any desire by the son or daughter to pull away from the overly invested adult is seen as a cataclysmic threat. In the pivotal moments when the teenager needs room to learn how to live life, the threatened parent becomes more intent on controlling the teen's life. This creates a vicious circle of absorbing demands and angry withdrawal.

The enmeshed parent looks at every failure or problem in the adolescent's life and concludes, "See, she needs me! She can't make it without me!" If the teenager uses drugs, hangs out with the wrong crowd, or develops a destructive habit with food, gambling, sex, or anything else, the overly attentive parent feels even more justified in treating the fledgling adult like a little child. Rather than responsibly setting boundaries toward healthy change, the parent's involvement can become so intense that counselors like Kenneth Adams call it "emotional incest."[3]

When parents drift this far, confusion and anger reign in an adolescent's life. Though a son or daughter wants to have a good relationship with their parents, they also have a God-given urge to pull away. If one parent clamps down and insists on treating him or her like a child, the teenager will deeply resent the intrusion and implied distrust, and will not just distance themselves but rip themselves away. The smothering parent insists what he's doing is pure love, but the teenager feels condemned, demeaned, and despised. He or she cannot grow deep roots or strong wings in such an environment.

Any smothering relationship—with a child, a spouse, a friend, a parent, a coworker, a boyfriend or a girlfriend—may be fueled by a God-given desire for closeness, but it arrests healthy and necessary development of the individuals as well as the relationship. The job of parents isn't just to ensure that their kids make the right choice for the moment; it is to help them acquire the insight and skill to make good decisions for the rest of their lives. That's a much bigger goal. It makes teaching, feedback, and internalizing values far more important than just telling teenagers what to do. It demands "loving release."

When the young adult walks out the door to go to college, enter the workforce, or get married, he or she still has a lot of growing up to do, but the self-perception and skills gained in adolescence provide a strong foundation for a successful life. Instead of celebrating a child's individual identity and responsibility, enmeshed parents feel threatened by both the process and the goal of their child's growth into adulthood. The power of their influence runs so deep that their children never develop a sense of identity that is separate from their parents' identity.

At Some Point, We Have to Grow Up

As Maria (from this chapter) learned, our past often explains the present, and our past isn't our past if it's affecting our present. If enmeshed adults had developed a vibrant, strong sense of self in adolescence, and if they had gained a sense of confidence and competence apart from their parents, they would be less likely to be dominated by or seek to control the people around them. But when we haven't experienced "good enough" parenting during those all-important years, adults of any age can realize significant developmental problems in their most important relationships.

In many ways, our fundamental misunderstanding of love stems from having our emotional and relational progress blocked as adolescents. The resulting insecurity created a sense of desperation that drove us to the extremes of isolation (to avoid the risk of being hurt again), or enmeshment (to find the closeness we crave). If we're not attentive and determined, we pass on our developmental issues to our kids, and they may pass them on to their children.

Some of us don't realize that we have fallen into the trap of counterfeit love until we're parents or grandparents. But no matter when the lights come on, it's important to get the message and begin the process of change.

If we remain needy and dependent people, we'll use others—even our children—for our sake instead of equipping them to love and be loved. Enmeshment poses as love but it actually feeds an empty heart at another's expense. And where children are concerned, enmeshment robs them of what they need most.

We're not saying this to heap shame on anyone, but to provide a point of understanding from which we can all take steps to break through and live differently.

In families with significant disorders and problems— perfectionists, narcissists, addicts, abusers, divorce, chronic disease, death—very few people receive adequate support to overcome the damage. Some cope better than others, but all members are deeply affected. Hurt, manipulation, and insecurity become "normal." So do the tendencies to hide and people-please.

Members of these families simply can't conceive of another way to live, but they have a nagging sense that life isn't what it should be. They desperately try to control others "for their own good," but the resentment they see in the eyes of those they try to control screams that something needs to change. They may not realize it, but they really long for a healthy independence in which people stay connected because they want to, not because they have to.

In a support group for people in tangled relationships, the facilitator explained these principles. One woman sat back in her chair and told the group, "It's crazy! I'm stuck as a thirteen-year-old!"

Many other people in the group chuckled in agreement. They, too, could identify their place in adolescence. They could begin to see what they had missed during those formative years.

One of the men in the group asked, "So then, what do we do now?"

Before the facilitator could respond, one of the group members spoke up: "I guess we need to learn how to become adults."

This wasn't a statement of shame, but of insight about the past and hope for the future.

No matter when a person faces adolescent developmental challenges—at age twelve or sixty-two—he has one consuming need: to grow up and acquire the identity, wisdom, and capabilities of an adult. Bondage always begs for freedom, and it's for freedom that Christ has come to set us free (Galatians 5:1)!

Your breakthrough demands moving beyond anything that is keeping you in bondage. And the past keeps many people imprisoned. The journey to freedom begins by recognizing where you are and how you got here, redefining what love is and isn't, and then learning to love and exercise healthy limits—all things we're exploring in this book. If your parents were more dysfunctional than delightful when you were growing up, just remember: you can put yourself in relationships today to learn the lessons you needed to learn back then. It's never too late.

We may have more habits, hang-ups, and memories to overcome, but we also have more resources today than we had when we were young. Back then we felt helpless and were clueless. Now we have a wide range of books, online resources, counselors, pastors, and recovery groups that can help us take bold steps forward. So don't get discouraged. Your change is coming! And through it all, you can count on God's goodness and grace to help you take the next step—no matter how frightening or difficult it may be.

THINK ABOUT IT . . .

1. How would you describe what needs to happen so that a thirteen-year-old child becomes a healthy, mature, competent young adult at the end of adolescence?

2. Which specific things can help to shape a person's sense of identity, discernment about who to trust, decision-making abilities, and sense of follow through?

3. List what you would consider to be characteristics of "good enough" parents.

4. In what ways did your parents (or guardians) provide a supportive environment so that you developed identity, trust, and responsibility? What was deficient?

5. In what ways have the deficiencies of your adolescence affected your key relationships as an adult?

6. Are there signs in your life today that you are stuck in adolescence? If so, what are they? What is your developmental age today?

7. What positive steps can you take to start making up for anything you failed to learn growing up?

CHAPTER 10

LEARNING TO TRUST WISELY

IT IS AN EQUAL FAILING TO TRUST
EVERYBODY AND TO TRUST NOBODY.

—*Thomas Fuller*

On her wedding day, Kim (chapter 1) was a vibrant, beautiful, self-confident young woman. But after several years of being dominated and oppressed in her marriage to Jasper, there wasn't much left in her. She had changed to a haggard, sad wife. When they dated, he was attentive, romantic, and affirming. To her dismay, soon after they walked down the aisle, Jasper seldom found a kind word to say to her. For the first few months, she felt confused and ashamed. She was convinced she had done something terribly wrong to receive such treatment. After a couple of years, however, she realized her marriage was more like a prison cell. She didn't feel loved or safe; rather, she felt trapped, hopeless, and alone. Kim wanted to see a counselor about her depression, but for months Jasper refused to let her go. Finally, he relented.

When Kim finally met the therapist, they talked about her need for a safe, secure place where she could process her feelings and grow strong again. In these conversations, the counselor talked about the importance of perceiving the truth about people and trusting wisely—trusting only those who have proven to be trustworthy. Kim looked forlorn as she reflected on the past few years, and remarked sadly, "My truster is broken."

She's not alone. People on either end of the spectrum of misconstrued love—enmeshed or isolated—have broken trusters. Why?

Trust is at the heart of every significant relationship. When trust is based on integrity and good will, it forms a solid foundation for the relationship to grow. When it is disordered, people feel terribly vulnerable and search for ways to protect themselves. The universal relational principle holds true: "If you can't trust, you have to control."

Trust: Our Foundation for Every Relationship

Trust is the first and foundational step of human development. It occurs during the first year of a child's life, even before communication with words. Infants depend on parents (or another adult caretaker) for food, shelter, attention, and affection. Even in the preverbal stage, children sense the relative love or chaos of the world around them. They instinctively know when their needs are being met and when something is missing.

When loving parents consistently meet an infant's needs, she develops a strong, healthy attachment to her parents and believes that her world is a safe place where she can live, explore, and thrive. To the extent the child feels unsafe, she feels insecure and instinctively learns to protect herself and control her world in any way she can.

The development of trust is tested through the relationships and experiences of adolescence. Those who have had the security of a loving, honest home environment have an upper hand in dealing with the challenges of raging hormones, the expectations of teachers and coaches, and the drive to pull away to carve out their own identities and chart a course for the rest of their lives. During these pivotal years, they desperately need to figure out who to trust, who to avoid, and what kinds of questions to ask in every relationship.

Teenagers gain wisdom about relationships by observing their friends in the hard world of trial-and-error. The urge to fit in causes many young people to discount their suspicions and embrace people who aren't good for them. They sometimes make friends with the wrong person, join the wrong group, and date the wrong boy or girl.

Knowing who to trust isn't easy. People don't wear name tags that say, "Danger! Don't trust me. I'm irresponsible!" And people are seldom purely evil or good. They come in all shades of gray, so one of the most important tasks of adolescence is to avoid the extremes of judgment and see people in their grayness. It takes much more wisdom to relate to people that way, but it's one of the chief skills young people need to learn.

The need for wisdom in relationships often clashes with the intrinsic desire to belong. Feeling alone and unwanted is one of the most painful experiences in any stage of life, but it's especially true for adolescents who long to be accepted by their peers. For teenagers, being accepted equals being valued. The need to belong to a group is so strong that it causes many young people to turn a blind eye to negative realities in the lives of those around them. In fits and starts, through painful trial-and-error, adolescents learn the hard truth that not everyone is trustworthy. They also learn they can't completely write off every person who makes a mistake—they have to gain enough savvy in relationships to live and thrive in the gray.

During these formative years, it's important for teenagers to learn to identify manipulation and uncover deception. They attempt to speak honestly and boldly about the flaws they see—in their friends and in themselves. They withhold trust from those who haven't proven they are trustworthy, and they don't feel guilty for not trusting them. They take small steps toward people to see how much and in what ways they can be trusted. And ultimately, if they've paid attention, they realize that trust is as valuable as gold but as fragile as glass, and they cherish it where they find it.

Discerning the Four Kinds of Trust

If a young person enters adolescence with disordered trust or fails to learn the hard lessons about relationships in adolescence, his or her development in every relationship will be stunted until it is remedied. People who can't trust feel compelled to control both situations and people. Their methods of control vary from pleasing to dominating, or perhaps avoiding any risk of meaningful connection.

The three disordered patterns of trust are blind trust, passive distrust, and aggressive distrust. If we can identify these patterns in our lives, we have a far better opportunity to take steps to change and cultivate the fourth kind of trust—wise trust. Let's consider each one:

Blind trust—the heroes

In tension-filled families, people look for any possible way to deal with pain, fear, and insecurity. For some, the truth about the people they love is too threatening, so they close their eyes to the chaos. To cope with the overwhelming problem of trying to relate to untrustworthy people, they choose to trust them anyway. In fact, they use trust as a bargaining chip in an attempt to manipulate others. Their intuitive thinking is: *I'll trust you, and then you'll owe me.* People who trust blindly are naïve and gullible, ready to believe obvious lies to avoid facing the hard truth. They usually wear the cape of a hero.

The goal of "blind trusters" is to win approval and avoid

conflict by pleasing angry people and controlling those who are out of control. This is the classic codependent who shuts her eyes to her husband's addiction, excusing him and picking up the slack in the home, and feeling powerful and needed when she fixes his problems (or thinking she's fixing them).

The person who trusts blindly controls others by preventing them from suffering the consequences of their behavior. The hero also believes the best despite all the evidence otherwise—and even when everyone else sees the painful truth. Blind trusters are usually very assertive in helping, fixing, and rescuing. Their emotions tend to gyrate wildly from rage at the irresponsible person to the ecstasy of having rescued that person again. "After all," the hero assures herself and anyone else who is watching, "what would he do without me?"

People who trust blindly define love as fixing a need— and the bigger the need, the better. This makes them feel more indispensable. They're often very perceptive about the needs of others, especially the needy one with whom they are enmeshed. They read that person's slightest facial expressions and hear minute changes in voice inflection, and then jump in to make that person happy. They are often pliable in the hands of powerful people, and they gravitate to the weak and needy who will appreciate their efforts to help them.

Nicole had been a sensitive, insecure child. When she met the young man who eventually became an abusive boyfriend, she felt sorry for him because he was an angry loner. Her friends stayed away from him, and they told her to watch out, but their warnings only made her feel more compassion for a boy no one trusted. When they started dating, she overlooked his callous self-absorption, his drug use, and the way he despised his mother. "If I love him enough," she told herself over and over again, "I know he'll change."

As he became more abusive, the scales on Nicole's eyes became thicker. She grew even more attached to him, more hopeful her love could change him, and more dominated by him. When she became pregnant, she finally saw what it would be like for a child to grow up with him as a father. The shock of this realization gave her the courage to move away, but even then, she often thought of going back to him. It took a long time and the consistent input of new, wise friends to help her see how foolish she had been to trust an abuser.

Passive distrust—the turtles

Blind trusters fully believe they have the power to change the life of an irresponsible, needy person, but people who are passively distrustful don't harbor such hopes. They've given up on getting close or making a difference in anyone's life. They're unable or unwilling to trust anyone, so they avoid any risk of intimacy.

Their goal in relationships is to give in or get away. They'll leave the room to avoid interaction, or if they stay, they hide behind a magazine or in front of a computer. They're terrified of powerful, dominating people, so they act like turtles, pulling into their shells at the slightest sign of a threat.

We might conclude that "passive distrusters" don't control anyone, but that's not the case. They rigidly control people's access to them, keeping them at a safe distance so they can't be hurt. They avoid conflict at all costs, but if it happens, they become easily flustered and give in to demands immediately to end the painful conversation.

These people define love as the absence of tension, not the presence of intimacy, affection, and trust. They relate to others with small talk and inconsequential facts, and they avoid potentially volatile topics like religion or politics that might create disagreement. Their identity has been crushed by people in their past. They may be so emotionally repressed that they aren't aware of the vast storehouse of painful emotions locked in their hearts. Even the slightest feelings of hurt, anger, or fear make them feel vulnerable and out of control—emotions they spend their lives trying to avoid.

In her relationship with Jasper, Kim had developed passive distrust. Before she married Jasper, she had been full of life. She was confident in relationships, laughed easily, and had a strong sense of purpose. Gradually, Jasper's incessant criticism took its toll. She became a shell of her former self, second-guessing every idea, berating herself for wanting to leave her husband, and feeling abandoned by God.

Kim had tried to talk to Jasper about her feelings, but his anger left her mush-brained and jelly-legged. He'd even convinced her that it was entirely her problem!

Like many turtles, she was susceptible to depression

because she'd lost hope that life could ever be good again. When she met with the counselor, her insights were a light in Kim's dark world.

Aggressive distrust—the field marshals

Rather than withdrawing, as passive distrusters do, some people react to the chaos around them by concluding, "I'm *never* going to let anyone hurt me again!" They don't trust anyone but themselves, and their coping strategy is to always be one-up, to win at all costs, and to take charge of every situation. They act like field marshals, commanding people and demanding compliance. They may use intimidation, positions of power, stealth, and knowledge to achieve these aims and to dominate those around them. They're skilled manipulators, sometimes alternating fierce condemnation with lavish praise to keep other people (typically heroes and turtles) off balance.

These people thrive on conflict—as long as they don't compete with people who are stronger than they are. They're never wrong, always in charge, and often have even sharper communication skills when the chips are down. They define love as "me in power and you in compliance." As long as their position isn't threatened, they can be quite sociable and gracious. In fact, this kind of person can be described as a blend of charm and venom. It's not pathological to be a strong leader, but there's something very wrong about using power to dominate instead of loving, serving, and looking out for the interests of others.

In the stories in this book, several people exhibit aggressive distrust. Jasper insisted on dominating Kim. For him, intimidation wasn't just an occasional flare-up—it was a daily habit, and he never came to her to ask for forgiveness. He was absolutely sure he was right in crushing her spirit into the dust. Nicole's boyfriend didn't have a respected position of authority, but he used Nicole's blind trust to dominate her in every way—physically, emotionally, sexually, and relationally. Before she came to her senses, he insisted that she ask for permission about where she was going each day. Phil's mother intimidated everyone in the family, but those on the outside never saw it. To outsiders, she was a beautiful, well-spoken woman. She could be the most charming person in the world, which disarmed Phil and made him feel all the more defenseless when she attacked.

Heroes are attracted to field marshals because they hope they can meet the demands and win approval from an authority figure. Turtles are attracted to field marshals, but for a very different reason: they want someone to tell them what to do, where to go, and how to act each day. As long as heroes and turtles obey, they can feel relatively certain they won't incur the field marshal's wrath—but then, they never really know for sure.

Wise trust—the adults

Insecurity drives people to use their God-given strengths in harmful ways. If heroes were emotionally strong and secure, they'd delight in helping others without any strings attached.

Field marshals would be leaders without using praise and intimidation to manipulate. And turtles would still be good listeners who were sensitive and humble, but they wouldn't be shackled by fear.

People who trust wisely have learned to be shrewd observers of the human condition. They aren't shocked when someone disappoints them, and they don't overreact to relatively small offenses. They are discerning but kind. They are cautious in taking risks in relationships, and they have the skills to take incremental steps of trust. Their goal is genuine attachment appropriate to the nature of the relationship—not enmeshed or isolated. They value honesty, mutual respect, and clear communication.

"Wise trusters" sometimes take steps to control people and their surroundings, but not out of pathological weakness. They've learned to set limits on their involvement so they can say yes when they want to and no when they need to. In conflict, they don't run away, give in too quickly to escape the uncomfortable moment, or use the difficulty to dominate the other person. They exhibit patience and persistence, pursuing resolution with honesty and taking responsibility for their part in the problem.

People who have learned the art of trusting wisely define love as "nonpossessive warmth." For them, love is caring for others with no strings attached. It means desiring the best for the other and always speaking the truth for everyone's benefit.

Paradoxically, not everyone feels comfortable relating to wise, strong, secure people. Those who trust blindly don't feel needed, and when they try to fix a wise person's problems, they feel rejected if the secure person resists their manipulative attempts. Those who are passive and refuse to trust feel pressured by the wise person's honesty, even if the wise one is very circumspect and inoffensive. And those who are aggressive feel threatened by the wise person who refuses to be cowed by intimidation.

Learning to Trust Wisely

Anyone can learn to trust wisely, but it takes a process combining insight, courage, encouragement, and trial-and-error—the same process an adolescent takes to become mature. Quite often, the first steps are incredibly difficult. Change is not easy for people who have lived their whole lives one way, even if their rigid assumptions about how relationships work have been wrong.

Several of the people in our stories have made remarkable progress from mistrust to wise trust. When a crisis forced them to take stock of their lives, they saw the destructive patterns and took steps to change. They began listening to good counsel and observed healthy relationships through new, clear lenses. They've demonstrated tremendous courage in their pursuit of love, respect, and trust and are now wonderful examples to others.

Those who trusted blindly began to ask more questions, be more skeptical of an irresponsible person's assurances, and value a person's deeds instead of believing empty words. Nicole's friends and parents recognized how untrustworthy and destructive her boyfriend was, but she couldn't see it. Every attempt they made to speak the truth drove her deeper into his clutches, wanting to defend him, because she felt threatened by any questions about his credibility or love.

When she got pregnant and moved away, her head began to clear. At first, she had only vague suspicions that he wasn't good for her. Her new friends and a counselor began to chip away at her rock-hard belief that he really loved her. She began to observe relationships in which couples respected each other, valued each other's opinions, and worked out disagreements without being mean, manipulative, or intimidating. It finally dawned on her that she was in a mess, and that this relationship was something other than love.

Nicole then did what most blind trusters do: she steadfastly refused to trust anybody. She became suspicious of even her most loyal friends and her parents. Her counselor had seen this before, and she helped Nicole take steps toward the middle. Nicole learned to ask good questions, to look for patterns of behavior, and to value people who treated her with respect.

The transformation has been remarkable. The deep wounds have largely healed, and after a while, she even took the risk to accept a date and begin a relationship with a young man who loved her without controlling her. Today, they are married and have three children. Nicole is a beacon of hope to young women who are escaping abusive relationships.

When people withdraw into a passive shell, they must realize they've protected themselves at the expense of real relationships. When Kim first met with a counselor, she tried to focus their conversations on her depression. She was very hesitant to discuss her relationship with Jasper because she knew he didn't want her to see the counselor in the first place. He would be furious if he knew she "betrayed" him by "blaming" him for her depression.

The counselor soon saw through her resistance and asked some penetrating questions. Kim felt safe enough to crack the door open, and soon shared more freely about her dilemma. The counselor helped Kim to draw on lessons she had learned in healthy relationships while growing up, and she regained perspective fairly quickly. She then faced the problem of how to cope with daily relational abuse and spiritual oppression.

Kim remembered how she had been wise and strong when she related to difficult people before she married Jasper, and she was determined to stand up to his intimidation. The counselor did several role-plays with her to help her prepare, and finally, she took the step.

In response, Jasper used one of his favorite intimidation tactics: he accused Kim of being unfaithful to him. Instead of wilting in fear, Kim found the courage to speak up, stand her ground, and tell him that she had never been unfaithful. And she didn't stop there. She told him she felt angry and sad that he would accuse her without any evidence. She went on to tell him that she wanted a respectful relationship with him and that she wasn't going to cave in to his intimidations any longer.

The counselor had warned Kim to expect Jasper to blow up, and she was right: it was Mount Saint Helens all over again! Jasper was furious. He yelled, accused, and tried to belittle Kim in every way that had worked before. Internally, Kim felt terrified, but she was prepared. She sat up straight in her chair, looked him in the eyes, and said, "If you want to resolve this issue, I'd be happy to talk with you when you can be civil." Jasper cursed her and stomped out of the room.

So far, this story doesn't have a happy ending. Kim has sought to reframe her relationship with her husband, trying to be consistently strong without being vindictive. She has, by her own admission, made mistakes—sometimes caving in to Jasper's intimidation and sometimes blowing up at him. Though she has gained some ground in the journey to find herself again, Jasper forbids her to see the counselor, and he hasn't changed much at all.

People who aggressively insist on being one-up in every relationship thrive on power and despise weakness. They're often the last to fall, but they hit hard. Jasper is certainly one of these people, as is Phil's mother. The hope for them, and for any of us, is to see their pattern of behavior for what it is.

The turning point for dominating, intimidating people is often a cataclysmic event. They usually exude supreme confidence. Difficulties don't generally throw them off track. In fact, they thrive on problems because they can prove themselves again as the dominant person in the family or company.

Sooner or later, however, they may experience a tragedy that forces them to face the cold, hard reality about their hidden flaws. In their case, the drive to dominate covers up a deep sense of insecurity, but they've buried the feeling so deep that they may not even be aware it's there. They're not hopeless, though. In fact, their drive can propel them to uncover their pain and find new ways to relate to others. Instead of intimidating people and treating them as stepping-stones to success, they can slow down, listen, serve, and value others.

Wisdom from the Example of Jesus

The steps to wise trust aren't easy, but with understanding and support, we can learn to transform the pattern of trust that has shackled us for a lifetime. Our growth into wise trust will require diligent pursuit and thoughtful observation of other people in relationships. One additional source of wisdom that we don't want to overlook is the example of Jesus.

When we look at the life of Jesus, we see him as the epitome of wise trust in the ways he related to people. He shrewdly observed people; he spoke the truth no matter how people might react; he offered relationship without manipulation. Let's look at a few examples of Jesus' strength and wisdom in relating to people.

• He always moved toward people to offer them a relationship based on honesty, humility, and trust, but his desire to demonstrate love didn't blind him to the reality that many people wouldn't accept his offer. Even as he proved his deity to the people, many scoffed at him. John tells us, "Now while he was in Jerusalem at the Passover festival, many people saw the signs he was performing and believed in his name. But Jesus would not entrust himself to them, for he knew all people. He did not need any testimony about mankind, for he knew what was in each person" (John 2:23–25). Jesus had no false illusions about people.

• He didn't wring his hands and hope that evil would go away. When the time was right, Jesus took action against injustice and openly opposed people who were harming others and defaming the honor of God. Remember the moneychangers in the temple? When Jesus found people selling livestock and treating God's house as a place of business, "he made a whip out of cords, and drove all from the temple courts, both sheep and cattle; he scattered the coins of the moneychangers and overturned their tables. To those who sold doves he said, 'Get these out of here! Stop turning my Father's house into a market!'" (John 2:15–17). He wasn't intimidated by powerful, pushy people.

• People had many expectations for Jesus, but he had a clear identity and purpose that guided his response to their demands. At one point, he healed so many people and became so popular that the disciples were sure they should stay in that location for a long time. But Jesus told them, "I must proclaim the good news of the kingdom of God to the other towns also, because that is why I was sent" (Luke 4:43). So he moved on with his traveling ministry. His first priority was the Father's will, not the desires of others, even his closest friends and family.

• He wasn't emotionally needy, so he didn't jump into committed relationships too quickly. He chose those who would be his closest friends only after spending time with them, observing them, and praying all night for his Father's guidance. Luke wrote, "One of those days Jesus went out to a mountainside to pray, and spent the night praying to God. When morning came, he called his disciples to him and chose twelve of them, whom he also designated apostles" (Luke 6:12–13).

• Jesus offered love and respect to people, and he let them make their own choices about a relationship with him. He wasn't a compulsive fixer. He offered healing to a man who had been sick for many years, asking him, "Do you want to get well?" rather than making assumptions. Wherever Jesus went, he told people about the kingdom of God and invited them to respond in faith. Some did; many didn't.

One day, a wealthy young man asked Jesus how to be saved. Jesus could tell that this man didn't come with a humble heart, so he told the young man to give up the things he valued most—the treasured possessions that were clogging his heart and preventing him from humbly accepting God's offer of forgiveness and love. Luke paints the picture for us: "When [the man] heard this, he became very sad, because he was very wealthy. Jesus looked at him and said, 'How hard it is for the rich to enter the kingdom of God! Indeed, it is easier for a camel to go through the eye of a needle than for someone who is rich to enter the kingdom of God'" (Luke 18:23–25). When the man walked away, Jesus didn't run after him and beg him to come back. He didn't lower his standards to suit the man and win his acceptance.

In all these instances (and throughout the gospel narratives), Jesus was observant, realistic, kind, and honest. He was willing to enter a relationship with anyone—even the most despised and rejected people of his day. He knew what was in people's hearts, so he knew who to trust and who to watch out for. He was strong, wise, and trustworthy and able to stand against the injustice, abuse, and oppression of the weak by the powerful.

Trust in Our Most Important Relationship

As we grow in our understanding of love and learn to trust wisely in our human relationships, we may discover that it's time for a makeover of our relationship with God. Our early life experiences powerfully shape our perceptions of life and how we trust or mistrust people. As we gain new perspective about the nature of trust in our most important human relationships, we also need to consider how our perception of God might be distorted.

The way we view our parents often determines how we view God. If our parents were strong and loving, we have a head-start in believing that God is great and good. If our parents were distant, we may surmise that God isn't very interested in us either. And if our parents were smothering and dominating, we may believe that we can never do enough to please God.

At first, we may feel terribly shaken when we realize we have trusted God just as foolishly or reluctantly as we have trusted the people around us. We may feel worse if we realize we have demanded that God prove himself trustworthy. Yet in time, we'll see that the kind of relationship God offers—with an open hand and a full heart—is far more wonderful than we ever imagined. Our growth must begin with a true assessment of where we are.

People who blindly trust untrustworthy people and rescue needy people often believe that it's God's job to rescue them from any difficulty. They pray, and they expect an answer. After all, the needy people in their lives don't even have to ask for help—the heroes just kick into gear to meet their needs. So, God (the ultimate Fixer in their opinion) should be just as quick to answer. When he doesn't, they get angry. Their unrealistic expectations of God cause them to feel terribly betrayed.

People who have passively withdrawn from relationships with powerful people may go to church, sing the songs, and read their Bible, but they see God as very distant and disengaged. The idea of a personal relationship with such a powerful being is painful to them. Like every other relationship in their lives, they prefer to keep God at arm's length: *I'll leave you alone if you don't bother me.*

And those whose lack of trust has caused them to try to dominate everyone and everything see God as either a powerful partner or a threat. Some of them are sure God will make them even more powerful. They focus on God's many promises of blessing and miss all the examples of Christ's humility and kindness.

As we become aware of our patterns of mistrust, we will need to make changes in order to grow in our friendship with God. Some of us will need to find the courage to approach him more boldly as we gradually grasp more of his love. Some of us will be humbled because we desperately need to be forgiven for how we've hurt others who God loves. It all starts with honesty about our perceptions, our hopes, and our hurts.

God has given us the great privilege of a relationship with

him—to be known by him and to know and trust him as he really is. King David endured much loneliness and insecurity during his lifetime, but when he reflected on the true character of God, he could honestly say: "Yes, my soul, find rest in God; my hope comes from him. Truly he is my rock and my salvation; ... I will not be shaken.... Trust in him at all times, you people; pour out your hearts to him, for God is our refuge" (Psalm 62:5–8). We, too, can share in his knowledge and trust in God.

THINK ABOUT IT . . .

1. In what ways is trust incredibly valuable, and in what ways is it terribly fragile?

2. How was your ability to trust wisely shaped by your childhood experiences? By your adolescent experiences?

3. Which of the four trust profiles best describes your approach to people? Explain your answer.

4. What are the steps a person with your trust profile needs to take to learn to trust more wisely?

5. Which characteristic of the way Jesus trusted was affirming or surprising to you?

6. What are the parallels between your expectations in relationships with people and your expectations in your relationship with God?

CHAPTER 11

BALANCING OUR RESPONSIBILITIES

YOU MUST TAKE PERSONAL RESPONSIBILITY. YOU
CANNOT CHANGE THE CIRCUMSTANCES, THE SEASONS,
OR THE WIND, BUT YOU CAN CHANGE YOURSELF.
THAT IS SOMETHING YOU HAVE CHARGE OF.

—Jim Rohn

"I'm learning to treat my husband with respect," Bethany (from chapter 1) told her friend. Well aware that Rick's porn addiction threatened to wreck his marriage to Bethany, the friend looked at her wide-eyed; she never expected Bethany to use the words *respect* and *my husband* in the same breath.

Bethany saw the expression on her friend's face and laughed. "I'm not saying that I approve of what he's been doing or the fact that he blames me for it," she explained. "But I'm committed to being an adult and letting him experience the consequences of his choices. Instead of me feeling guilty for his decisions and treating him like a disobedient child, I'm respecting his position as an adult. I'm determined to let him take responsibility and see how he handles it."

Her friend understood. Bethany was taking big steps. She was assigning appropriate responsibility and setting boundaries for herself.

Our understanding of love determines the scope, focus, and intensity of our sense of responsibility. If we think love is being a hero to needy people, we'll take responsibility for their feelings and behavior. If we believe love is being one-up, we'll dominate everyone around us and tell them what they are "supposed" to do. And if we perceive love as the absence of any risk, we'll allow only superficial connections and avoid steps toward truth and love.

Whether we're on the enmeshed or the isolated end of the continuum, we have a profound imbalance of responsibility. We're overly responsible about some things but irresponsible about others. If we fail to see this imbalance in our thoughts and actions, our compulsions will remain unchecked. We'll continue seeking to control others by smothering them, dominating them, or avoiding them. We'll stay locked into relationships of counterfeit love. We'll keep rolling along with no change—and no idea that change is even needed. As we gain insight, however, we'll learn to redefine our responsibilities.

What Is Our Responsibility?

As it does for many other challenging areas of life, the Bible teaches sound principles for understanding the scope and limitations of our responsibility—what we are and are not responsible for. In his letter to the Galatians, Paul addresses our responsibilities to those around us.

First, we have an obligation to shine a light on irresponsible, harmful behavior: "Brothers and sisters, if someone is caught in a sin, you who live by the Spirit should restore that person gently. But watch yourselves, or you also may be tempted" (Galatians 6:1). In our relationships with addicts, prodigals, or people who use volcanic anger to intimidate, for example, Paul instructs us to speak up—not to yell and condemn, but to confront in order to "gently restore" the person. Sometimes, all it takes is a short conversation to say, "Hey, here's what I see in your life. I know that's not how you want to treat people. It's time to change."

But in chronically disruptive families, the web of deceit, selfishness, and manipulation is strong, and sinful patterns of thought and action are deeply ingrained. In these cases, we may need more batteries to shine the light on irresponsible behavior! Even then, God wants us to stand firm so that we don't give up or overreact.

That's the temptation. Some of us are tempted to smother the person with directions and offer so much assistance that we rob him of personal responsibility. Others are tempted to use fierce scowls and harsh words to browbeat people into submission. Still others are tempted to avoid any hint of conflict, so they never say a word, hoping the person will change on his own or that someone else will talk to him. So, the first directive in Paul's letter is to notice destructive attitudes and actions in people's lives, name these things in honest, grace-filled conversations, and avoid the temptation to smother, intimidate, or bail.

Second, the difficulties in people's lives are often too much for them to bear alone, and they need our help. These struggles may result from a wide range of causes: their sins, the sins of others, natural disasters, economic collapse, accidents, and unexpected events. Whatever the source, God wants us to pitch in to help.

Paul writes, "Carry each other's burdens, and in this way you will fulfill the law of Christ" (Galatians 6:2). The image in this verse is of an overloaded ox cart with a wheel that's fallen off. One person can't pick up the heavy load and put the wheel back on. It takes the help of others to raise the cart and repair the wheel so the person can get going again.

Helping those in need fulfills Christ's command to "love your neighbor as yourself." There are people in our lives today whose burden is too heavy for them to carry. Our God-given responsibility and privilege is to set aside our comfort, follow the example of Jesus, and help them.

But Paul, the shrewd pastor, understood that some of us look for opportunities to help so that we can be heroes.

Helping in this way actually hurts the person. So he balances his instruction about responsibility by writing, "If anyone thinks they are something when they are not, they deceive themselves. Each one should test their own actions. Then they can take pride in themselves alone, without comparing themselves to someone else, for each one should carry their own load" (Galatians 6:3–5).

Do we think we're Superman or Wonder Woman who can take on everyone else's responsibilities? We're not. Do we see ourselves as field marshals who need to tell stupid, weak people what to do with their lives? We're not. Are we so timid and fearful that our greatest hope is to avoid any interaction that includes the risk of disagreement? We need not be that afraid.

The message of Paul's passage (and the message of this book) is to step back and take a good, hard look at ourselves. If we are controlling people by enabling sinful behavior (assuming responsibilities that rightfully belong to them) or dominating (not allowing them to be responsible or continually telling them what they must do), that's not love. One way we can discern our true motives is whether we compare ourselves with others. Do we long for more praise or power? Are we jealous when others get more applause or a promotion? These are good indicators that our helping isn't coming from strength and love, but from insecurity and the compulsion to control.

Paul says that our responsibility for others stops at the point where they should own their choices and the consequences—that's their rightful load. Each person has to carry the responsibility for his thoughts, attitude, responses to people, discipline to get work done, and so on. Whenever we do these things for them, we're stepping over the line and assuming responsibility that doesn't belong to us. That's when helping becomes hurting.

Jesus cared for people without smothering them, without controlling them. He corrected the false teachings of the religious leaders, but not to punish them. He gave tirelessly at times, but he retreated with his followers to recharge his emotional engines. He knew when to say yes and when to say no. He clearly understood love and boundaries. He wasn't confused about the limits of responsibility. His compassion led him to help, but he never crossed the line and imposed himself on anyone. At the right times, with the right people, and in the right ways, he chose to act.

Acquiring Your Skills

One of the most important things we can learn during the adolescent years is to define the limits of our responsibility. Teenagers may not see the need to study, brush their teeth, do their chores, come home on time, limit their time online, and fulfill their other assignments. But all of these things—the ones they enjoy and the ones they detest—are important if they're going to become fully functioning adults. Their parents are given the thankless job of helping to shape these habits. Too often, insecure moms and dads are either smothering and overprotective, detached and lenient, or harsh and demanding, and their children fail to develop an adult perspective on responsible behavior.

Like our sense of identity and the ability to trust wisely in relationships, learning the principles of responsibility can happen at any age—in fact, we *must* learn these things, no matter how far behind we may be. Learning to assign appropriate responsibility is one of the secrets to living and loving well. This means that we have to notice what is happening around us, determine what is and is not appropriate, and then clearly define a plan so that we aren't overly responsible or irresponsible any longer.

Both the spouse of a porn addict and the parent of an alcoholic need to realize that denying the problem doesn't solve anything. At the same time, blowing up and demanding change seldom produces lasting results either. Instead, if you find yourself in a strained, deceptive relationship, you need to first accept the responsibility to be honest with yourself and with God. Then you can offer a path forward with the other person based on truth, trust, and respect. If that person agrees to move ahead, there's hope; but if not, you shouldn't go back and resort to manipulation to control the person's behavior. Author and pastor Lewis B. Smedes has said, "The highest respect you can show people is to let them take responsibility for their own actions."[1]

To help in the process of assigning appropriate responsibility, Alcoholics Anonymous adopted a prayer by the theologian Reinhold Niebuhr. It's known as the Serenity Prayer. Most of us are familiar with the first couple of lines, but the longer version adds to our understanding of the scope and limitations of personal responsibility:

> God, grant me the serenity to accept the things I cannot change; courage to change the things I can; and wisdom to know the difference.
>
> Living one day at a time; enjoying one moment at a time; accepting hardships as the pathway to peace; taking, as He did, this sinful world as it is, not as I would have it; trusting that He will make all things right if I surrender to His Will; that I may be reasonably happy in this life and supremely happy with Him forever in the next. Amen.[2]

We need God's help—usually given through his Word and his people—to figure out the difference between a friend or family member's crushing burden and his backpack. The burden they may need some help with; the backpack they can handle on their own.

We also need God's wisdom to know which of our own weights we carry each day are burdens requiring the help of others and those we need to carry ourselves. If we didn't learn those things in adolescence, we can still learn them now.

Necessary Adjustments

Many years ago, I (Pat) flew back to Austin with a friend after attending a conference. On the flight, I complained about the stress I was feeling. She asked about my family background, and after I told her about the alcoholism, anger, and manipulation, she looked at me and said, "Pat, you're irresponsible."

I was stunned. I had lived every moment of my life so that no one would ever say those words to me. Instantly, I felt like a cornered bobcat. I was furious, but I tried to avoid biting off her head. Instead, I took a deep breath and asked, "What do you mean? Maybe you misunderstood what I was saying."

She smiled and responded, "No, I understood very well. You're very dedicated to doing a great job at work and taking care of the people around you. In fact, you're too dedicated to those things. You don't take care of yourself—especially your heart."

In my mind, I was thinking, *I have no clue what she's talking about*, but I didn't want to appear dumb, so I simply said, "Tell me more."

She smiled again, "You don't understand, do you?"

"I guess not," I answered. So for the next hour, I got a crash course in the destructive power of enmeshment, and I learned how I had been out of balance: taking responsibility for fixing others' problems instead of letting them learn from the consequences, and not taking responsibility to resolve the hurt, anger, and fear in my own heart.

For the first time, I realized it's not a virtue to thrive on feeling needed. I was on the verge of burnout, but until that conversation, my solution was to be even more "responsible" by enabling, fixing, and being a hero. It was a wake-up call—the beginning of a long process of discovery and change.

To find the right balance of responsibility, some of us need to say less, some need to say more; some need to sit down, some need to stand up; some need to say no, some need to say yes. How do we know which steps toward change are right for us to take? It depends on who we are. People in each category of mistrust need to make unique adjustments as they learn to deal with responsibility as adults.

For heroes

Those who trust blindly and are driven to please are overly responsible in taking care of others. But it's not the hero's job to make others happy and fix their problems. When heroes take a step back and look at their lives, they can observe the compulsive patterns of behavior, the obsessive thoughts, and the driving fear of not doing enough to be noticed. But heroes also exhibit a form of irresponsible behavior: they're so busy fixing others' problems that they don't deal with their own underlying issues—their hurt, fear, anger, and compulsions. Of course, for a long time, this warped sense of responsibility—both over and under—seems completely normal, right, and good.

As Phil realized this pathological pattern in his life, he told a close friend who was helping him walk through all this, "I thought being everybody's hero was the most noble thing in the world. I transferred all my people-pleasing strategies from my family to, well, . . . to everybody on the planet! I've lived for approval, but it was never enough. They didn't even have to ask for my help. I gave it whether they asked for it or not and whether they even needed it or not."

Phil's adjustments included a commitment to stop rushing to meet every need he noticed, saying no to certain requests for his help, and in fact, stopping to consider whether it would be good for him to help at all. Emotionally, he realized he had taken responsibility for others' sins and failures. For years, the shame and guilt had piled up and become a mountain. Foolishly, Phil had trusted people he should have had second thoughts about, and some of them had taken advantage of him.

As he gained more wisdom and strength, he was able to reframe his thinking and his choices. Gradually, his life became less cluttered with others' expectations and demands, and Phil stopped jumping to meet every need he encountered. He learned to relax and let others experience the consequences of their choices. "I'd always thought protecting them from the pain of their choices was the most loving thing I could do," he reflected, "but now I realize I was the biggest hindrance to their growth. All of my efforts to fix people were the problem, not the solution."

For turtles

Those who have tried to cope with chaos by withdrawing into a shell need to make very different adjustments than heroes and field marshals. Instead of hiding in fear, they need to move forward (timid at first, but steps nonetheless) toward people. They engage by asking questions, and they take the risk of sharing their opinions. Instead of answering every question with, "I don't know" or "It doesn't matter to me," they find the courage to say, "Actually, I like pepperoni. If you don't mind, let's get that on our pizza." (And if you think that's an odd illustration of the steps these people need to take, you probably don't know any of them.)

In the past, to end conflict as quickly as possible, turtles have instantly caved in to others' demands and admitted fault when they weren't really to blame. Now, they find new strength to speak the truth—maybe with a heart full of fear, but they say what they really believe in difficult conversations. As they come out of their shells, they make a few meaningful connections with people they've brushed by for years. At first, they hesitatingly open their hearts and take the risk of being hurt. Sometimes, they're disappointed that others aren't as kind as they hoped they'd be, but they also find real friendships and true joy in knowing and being known.

When Kim finally went to a counselor to talk about her relationship with Jasper, she was very confused. Jasper had convinced her that she was responsible for the problems in their marriage. She was like a sponge soaking up the blame, taking responsibility for Jasper's anger. In their first session, she told the counselor, "He wouldn't be so angry if it wasn't for me. I just know it." Then she broke down in tears.

Over time, Kim realized she was far out of balance in her concept of responsibility. She'd been accepting the blame for Jasper's feelings and behavior, yet hadn't been honest about the cesspool of painful emotions swirling in her heart. As Kim gained insight about her marriage, she began to clarify responsibilities. She was finally able to grieve the hurts instead of burying them, start the process of forgiving Jasper, and speak the truth to him about his oppressive behavior. He didn't take it very well, but she realized it was the only path to a relationship based on trust and respect.

For field marshals

People who have repeatedly stepped over the line by aggressively dominating others have, like heroes and turtles, neglected the development of their own hearts. In that way, they were irresponsible. Their compulsion to win at all costs has come at a steep price in strained relationships, resentment self-righteousness, and unrelenting but deeply buried insecurity. To stop playing the role of field marshal, they need to make a few changes. A new set of responsibilities includes:

- beginning to ask questions and listening to answers instead of barking orders
- letting others make their own decisions instead of telling them what to do
- speaking words of affirmation instead of using condemnation to intimidate
- speaking those words of praise without manipulative strings attached

People who have been driven to win at all costs never wanted to "let their slip show," so they seldom if ever admitted they're wrong. Now, with a new sense of security and taking the risk to trust that at least a few people will accept them for who they are, they begin to "confess their faults to one another." It's a huge step for these people, and wonderfully healing for everyone involved.

Carl was always at the top of his class, and he learned to use his intellect as a club to bludgeon people, including his wife, his kids, and those who reported to him at work. As long as they were in awe of his vast knowledge about every topic under the sun, he gave them a place in his life. But if anyone disagreed with him, missile attacks ensued! After his third divorce, Carl's children from his first marriage refused to speak to him any longer. Suddenly, his knowledge wasn't enough to give him the power he craved. He was devastated. He talked to Richard (the only friend he had left), and asked for help.

Richard was shocked. "You're asking me for advice?"

"Yeah," Carl moaned. "I've really messed up my life, and I don't know how to make it right."

Richard helped Carl begin to understand the difference between dominating people and respecting them. "Your responsibility," Richard explained, "is to listen. Ask questions, then shut up and listen."

This was a foreign concept to Carl, but Richard was kind enough to role-play conversations Carl could have with his college-age kids. In the weeks that followed, Richard coached Carl in taking responsibility for the damage he'd done to his kids, his wives, and his staff, and taught him some new communication skills. For a long time, Carl worked at shutting up and reflecting back what others were saying to him instead of correcting them. But after a while, he realized he was seeing something he'd seldom seen in the past: another person's smile.

When heroes, turtles, and field marshals learn to act like adults, they experience more joy, freedom, and love than they ever dreamed possible. They learn to redefine the scope of responsibilities. They know there's a difference—a big difference—between being responsible for someone and being responsible to him. They realize they've taken responsibility for others' feelings, choices, and virtue, but now, things are different. They are only responsible to speak the truth in love and offer a path forward paved with truth and respect. They've given up on manipulating, begging, and fixing. They begin to genuinely connect with people. Sometimes, they get hurt and feel compelled to retreat to their old habits, but if they stay on track, they'll continue to discover deeper experiences of affection and deep connection with others who are trying to be adults too.

Find the Courage to Take Bold Steps

As has been mentioned, when we change, we shouldn't expect the people closest to us to stand up and cheer.

If we've been harsh or irresponsible, our loved ones will be skeptical because they've heard our promises to change so many times before. If we've been compulsive rescuers, they won't like us upsetting the status quo. Why would they? They're completely comfortable with our seemingly selfless efforts to fix their problems and meet all their needs.

When we pull back, they utter the epithet we've dreaded all our lives: they accuse us of being "so selfish!" We may waver at that point and give in to their expectations for a while, but even then, we'll know that the system is irreparably broken; we can't go on living the lie any longer.

As long as we're only dabbling in change—reading books, talking to friends, going to a support group once in a while—change isn't too threatening. But when we step into the lion's den to say no to someone who has lived by our yeses, or we speak up instead of cowering in fear, or we confess that we've hurt the people we love by intimidating them, we come face-to-face with the biggest challenge of our lives. At that moment, everything in us wants to run away. We have to find a way to stay on track until we break through.

Unstoppable is a movie based on actual events when an unmanned train got stuck in gear and sped along the tracks in Pennsylvania. It barrels through towns, crushes cars, and wrecks other trains along the way. Throughout the film, the two main characters try to figure out a way to stop the train before it reaches a sharp turn in the middle of a city. If it comes in too fast, it'll run off the tracks, hit an oil depot, and cause huge devastation. The two men fight against the plans of the railroad executives, the physics of the enormous power of the train, and their own fears, but eventually, they find a way to overcome its seemingly unstoppable momentum.

This story is a metaphor for our lives as we face the tremendous power of our entrenched bad habits and the rigid expectations of others. There are no easy answers. We have to keep fighting, working together, and trying different things until we discover a plan that works for us. Then we have to find the courage to take bold steps to make the plan a reality. There is no easy out, no quick solution, and no magic potion to change other people. Instead, we trust God to transform us, guide us, and help us in the process of growing into maturity.

The change in direction, though, begins with a single decision to change the course of our lives, much like the men in *Unstoppable* made the dramatic choice to try to stop the train.

At a moment in time, we say, "I'm not going in that direction any longer. I trust God to give me the wisdom and strength to live a different kind of life." And we mean it.

Bethany stopped feeling responsible for Rick's addiction. She made the decision to give him the responsibility for his behavior.

Jackson and Susan (chapter 1) had tried everything they knew to protect their son, Bill, from the consequences of his addiction, but enabling him had given them ulcers and made him even more irresponsible and selfish. They had rescued him dozens of times because they felt so guilty for being "bad parents," but now, as they saw reality more clearly, they traded their guilt for grief and let him choose his future.

Phil realized his heroic compulsion to control people who were out of control had driven him to be a hero for needy people, a field marshal over people who reported to him at work, and a weak, frightened turtle in response to a few intimidating people around him. When he finally saw the gravity of his problem, he knew he had to change practically everything in his life. He had to reframe his responsibilities in each relationship.

Rachel, who we also met in chapter 1, had to learn to show common respect to her teenager instead of spying on her. If she kept snooping, she'd lose the girl's trust. So instead, she opened the lines of communication so she and her daughter could talk about the things that matter. Rachel could help her daughter process all the craziness of adolescence and learn to act responsibly only if they talked openly.

Kim's situation is the most precarious. Standing up to an abuser is always risky. She got plenty of help from her counselor, but this train was flying down the wrong tracks! Her first attempts to take responsibility and speak the truth to Jasper met hostile defiance, but to her credit, she didn't back down and she didn't yell at him. In several hard confrontations, she looked him in the eye and said, "I want our relationship to be full of trust and respect, but we're not there. I'm willing to work on it. Are you?" Kim is serious about taking appropriate responsibility in her relationship with her husband and expecting him to respond in kind. We'll see how it turns out.

James had grown up feeling responsible for his father's reputation as a respected church leader, but his fears and self-doubts had shattered him. For a long time, he had vacillated between shame for being a bad son and rage at the pressure he felt from his dad. Finally, he concluded that he was responsible to be an honest and honorable man, but he had to let his father's reputation rest on its own merits. He unhooked himself from feeling responsible for the way the public saw his father.

Responsibility Has Limits

Responsibility and love are inextricably related. If we're overly responsible, we manipulate people to cover our insecurities and earn applause and power. If we're irresponsible and expect others to carry the load we should carry, we use them instead of loving them. One-up and one-down relationships may be common, but they're based on something other than genuine love and respect. We have to grow up, act like adults, and treat others with the respect they deserve—which means affirming the good in them as well as letting them be responsible for the consequences of their own choices.

In their seminal work, *Boundaries*, Henry Cloud and John Townsend wrote, "Knowing what I am to own and take responsibility for gives me freedom. If I know where my yard begins and ends, I am free to do with it what I like. Taking responsibility for my life opens up many different options. However, if I do not 'own' my life, my choices and options become very limited."[3]

Or, as Dirty Harry famously said, "A man's got to know his limitations."

THINK ABOUT IT . . .

1. What is the connection between our sense of identity, trusting wisely, and defining appropriate responsibilities?

2. Think about your most important relationships. What are some "burdens" in their lives you need to help your loved ones bear? Which emotional, financial, or other kind of "load" are you carrying that someone else should be shouldering? Which of your loads is someone carrying for you? Explain your answers.

3. In what ways are heroes overly responsible? In what ways are they irresponsible? What would balance look like?

4. In what ways are field marshals overly responsible? In what ways are they irresponsible? What would balance look like?

5. In what ways are turtles overly responsible? In what ways are they irresponsible? What would balance look like?

6. What can you expect from yourself and from those around you as you learn to live like an adult and assign appropriate responsibility? What will be some of the benefits? Is it worth it? Why or why not?

7. In what ways does making changes in your life feel like trying to stop a runaway train?

CHAPTER 12

SPEAKING THE HARD TRUTH

I LOVE YOU, AND BECAUSE I LOVE YOU, I WOULD
SOONER HAVE YOU HATE ME FOR TELLING YOU THE
TRUTH THAN ADORE ME FOR TELLING YOU LIES.

—Pietro Aretino

From the outside, Brittany and Mark seemed to have a very pleasant relationship. They went to church, attended Bible studies, and hung out with friends. Brittany's sister Liz was the only one who suspected something wasn't quite right in the couple's marriage. For months, Liz probed gently to see if Britt would "spill her guts," but she always insisted everything was fine. Finally, on a girls' weekend, Liz got her sister alone and asked bluntly, "Hey, I know you don't want to talk about it, but I think there's something wrong between you and Mark. Tell me what's going on."

Brittany tried to blow it off again, but Liz wouldn't let it go. After a long silence, Brittany told her, "You're right. For a long time I've felt like a widow. Mark pours himself into his career, and when he comes home, he watches sports. When I try to talk to him, he says he's too tired. I feel like a widow living with a stranger." She began to cry. After she dried her eyes, she continued, "I've loved him! I've given him all I've got, and he treats me like a used magazine."

"You've got to talk to him," Liz said with an appropriate blend of anger and compassion.

Brittany shrugged, "What's the use? He won't listen."

"If he won't listen to your heart," Liz stated defiantly, "you don't have a relationship. You never know until you try."

True love is based on honesty between two people. In a strained relationship, eventually we will have to speak the truth to the other person and confront the hard facts about past hurts, present expectations, and the possible future. Some people use confrontation as a way to dominate others, but probably more people avoid conflict at all costs. Sooner or later, we gain the wisdom, courage, and skills to speak the truth—not to intimidate, but to change the matrix of the relationship so it can be based on honesty and respect. That's the only way the relationship can be a source of authentic love.

And let's not be fooled. It's not like the other person hasn't noticed how we have changed and who we are becoming. When we begin to act like adults, we threaten the equilibrium of our key relationships. The people we are closest to have a vested interest in keeping us locked into our old roles, our old ways. If we've been compliant and willing to fix their problems in the past, they want us to keep it up until the day we die. If we've taken control by telling people what to do and where to go so they don't have to think for themselves, they feel very uncomfortable when we insist that they take responsibility for their choices. And if we've been withdrawn, weak, and invisible, they're shocked when we begin to express our preferences.

As we become stronger in our new adult identity, we realize (fairly quickly) that some of our relationships aren't what they need to be. We are no longer content to manipulate and pretend that a counterfeit is true love. Instead, we want to share a relationship based on trust and respect. One of the skills we need to acquire to accomplish this change, for this critical moment and for the rest of our lives, is the ability to confront appropriately.

We need to confront because most of the people in our key relationships won't like the changes we're making one bit. The people in our lives who will stand up and applaud our progress are our counselors, support group members, and wise friends who understand what we're doing. Most family members (and anyone else with whom we're enmeshed) will use whatever method they've used before—self-pity, rage, pleas, promises, silence—to manipulate us to go back to the way we were before.

Confrontation: Catalyst for Change, Invitation for True Love

To avoid hard choices in difficult relationships, people blind themselves to the faults of others and the damage they inflict, and then remain entangled in the relationship. Or if that doesn't work, they get as far away as possible from the person. But in most relationships, God wants us to grow strong instead of running away. He directs us to "speak the truth in love."

Sometimes, the truth *comforts*. Jesus spoke words of grace and gentleness to those who were broken and needy. But the truth also *confronts*. Jesus didn't hesitate to call the religiously oppressive leaders a "brood of vipers" and "whitewashed tombs." He didn't back away from saying what needed to be said—never with the motive of revenge, but always with the hope that the truth would correct and heal.

We might share the hope that truth will bring healing, but speaking the truth in an enmeshed relationship is still a frightening proposition. So we might ask, "Do I really need to confront that person? I don't think it will turn out well at all, and then there will be more damage to overcome."

We speak the truth for three reasons: First, in the integrity of our hearts, we obey God to speak truth and follow his leading to offer a path to reconciliation. Second, our honesty gives the other person an opportunity to face the hard facts of life and repent. Sometimes God works in incredible ways to change a heart that we thought was hardened beyond hope.

And third, confronting a person can give us more insight into the pathology of the relationship and reveal more hurt and fear than we've ever seen before. It may be a major step in our own healing.

When Phil came to a point of confronting his angry, demanding mother, he was under the illusion that she would instantly repent, and they would have the relationship he always wanted. When they talked, he was shocked when she blamed him for anything and everything wrong in the family. This shattering experience, though, cleared away Phil's delusions, surfaced far more hurt and anger, and provided an opportunity for him to grieve and forgive his wounds more fully. He explained, "It was one of the most significant things I've ever done in my life. In some ways, the conversation with my mother was a disaster, but in others, it was a source of light and healing. Finally, I knew the truth about my mother and her opinion of me. It hurt . . . a lot . . . but now I could live in truth. Paradoxically, it freed me from the chains of false expectations that my mother would ever really love me."

There are no guarantees when we speak the truth to people who have hurt us. Quite often, they respond in a predictably resistant way, and we walk away with our integrity and the reassurance that we've done what God asked us to do. But sometimes, a heart melts in the light of the truth we share, and the process of reconciliation begins. It's a beautiful thing when it happens. And it doesn't happen without confrontation.

Yes, Confrontation Is Threatening

Out of fear of confrontation, some people cling to the hope that the difficult person will magically change on his own, so they never take the step of speaking truth to him. Some avoid confrontation because they feel intense anger and believe they need to have "perfect peace" before they can have an honest conversation with someone who has abused or abandoned them. Others are paralyzed by the fear that addressing the reality of hurt and manipulation in the relationship will cause irreparable harm.

There are countless other excuses for avoiding a transparent and difficult conversation. A few of them are completely valid. When there is significant risk of physical violence, we need to avoid inflaming the person's wrath and exposing ourselves to danger. In these cases, a restraining order may be more appropriate than a conversation. Some women who have been abused or physically dominated by a boyfriend put themselves at risk by having a private talk with him. When the possibility exists that the confrontation could become violent, or if the person initiating the confrontation feels particularly weak and vulnerable, it's a good idea to have a third party, such as a counselor, attorney, or pastor, mediate the meeting.

Most of us, however, face risks that aren't physically threatening. We need to prepare ourselves for what we may encounter on the path ahead. Proverbs speaks clearly about relating to fools—people who are stubborn and demand their own way, even when their behavior hurts others. These passages give us backbone as we consider what it means to lovingly speak the truth to needy, absorbing people or harsh, demanding people:

- 13:17: "A wicked messenger falls into trouble, but a trustworthy envoy brings healing." Foolish people say things that hurt others instead of healing them.

- 14:9: "Fools mock at making amends for sin, but goodwill is found among the upright." Foolish people won't admit they're wrong.

- 18:2: "A fool finds no pleasure in understanding, but delights in airing his own opinions" (NIV1984). Foolish people don't listen to others, but they insist that we listen to them.

- 29:11: "A fool gives full vent to his anger, but a wise man keeps himself under control" (NIV1984). Foolish people sometimes explode in rage and use their anger to intimidate others.

How, then, should we respond to foolish people? Two proverbs seem to contradict each other, but they indicate that we need to be wise and selective in our approach:

- 26:4-5: "Do not answer a fool according to his folly, or you will be like him yourself. Answer a fool according to his folly, or he will be wise in his own eyes." There are times when we need to be silent and not get into an argument with a foolish person, but there are other times when we need to speak boldly and clearly to refute him. It takes wisdom to know the difference.

And it takes wisdom to confront with grace. Confrontation is not yelling, pointing a finger in people's faces, and accusing them of shameful acts. It can be accomplished without losing control or using manipulation. In fact, speaking the plain, unvarnished truth can be the most loving thing we can do for another person.

Principles for Speaking the Truth

Confronting someone who has hurt us is a very difficult and threatening task. When we actually walk into the room and see the person's face, we may become confused, shut down emotionally, or become violently angry. We may move toward resolution too quickly without being honest about the facts, or we may choose revenge instead of progress because "it's only fair."

Confrontations can be as minor as, "That hurt my feelings. Please don't say that again" after a one-time verbal jab. Or confrontations can address the most deeply rooted emotional issues in life. In either case, certain principles can be followed as a path of resolution in strained and broken relationships. Obviously, the less severe issues don't require as much preparation as more painful ones, so use discretion about the degree to which these principles are to be used. It's wise, however, to be overprepared instead of ill-prepared.

1. Be prepared.

That's the Boy Scout motto, and it needs to be the guiding principle for confrontations too. Preparation helps us to take control of our thoughts and behavior. As we think and reflect, we can determine what we really want in the relationship and how the confrontation can help us toward that goal. Preparation can also help us to develop realistic expectations about the other person's response. Many of us feel that if we speak the truth, the other person ought to repent immediately in sackcloth and ashes. That probably won't happen! At the other extreme, some of us expect (or fear) that we're locked in a hopeless relationship that will never change. This perspective is equally unrealistic because each of us has the power to at least change ourselves.

Preparation involves knowing how we typically respond in similar situations. One man typically becomes fierce and intimidating because he's afraid of losing control. A high school student makes flip, sarcastic remarks to prove she's not affected by her father's harsh criticism. A woman becomes emotionally paralyzed and gives in to whatever the other person wants. If we know our tendencies to dominate, escape, or rationalize, we have a much better chance of not giving in (as much). If we can anticipate how the other person may respond, we can walk through a few "what ifs" and be better equipped to respond as we wish.

We usually have tunnel vision and don't see our own behavior very clearly. So we benefit from wise, objective input from a trusted friend, professional counselor, pastor, or in some cases, a lawyer. A professional can give us the feedback we need to set our course properly and role-play the conversation. When the person we confront is particularly hostile or stubborn, or when legal action is being contemplated, we may want to invite a professional to mediate.

2. Major on the majors.

We may be able to list hundreds of offenses that have hurt us or bothered us, but a long list weakens our point. Weed it out until there are only a few issues (no more than two or three) to discuss. If a lot of wounds and instances of broken trust are truly significant, you can talk about a few during the first meeting. If these are successfully resolved, the others can be addressed later.

3. Set the agenda.

You can set up the meeting by calling to say, "I'd like to talk to you about our relationship. Can you meet me at ten o'clock Saturday morning to talk?" But be careful that you don't get pulled into a discussion about the issues at that point. Stay in control. If the person demands an explanation on the phone, say, "I don't want to talk about it right now. We can talk at length on Saturday."

When the meeting begins, don't be vague about the topic of conversation. Even though your stomach may be in knots and your mind is racing, state clearly what you see as the problem and communicate your desire to resolve the problem. Typically, the person you're confronting is at least as nervous as you are. (But he hasn't prepared like you have!) You can expect him to use whatever manipulative techniques he has used on you before: self-pity, anger, yelling, silence, blaming you for the whole problem, accepting all the blame just to end the meeting, and so on. He may try to get you off track by bringing up other problems. Many of us get confused and flustered at this point. To make sure you can keep on track with your goal for the meeting, take a written agenda with you. When you need to refocus your thoughts (and for some of us, that's immediately after we say hello), pull out the sheet and follow your plan.

4. Clarify what is said.

One of the most effective ways to confront someone is to "hold up a mirror" by repeating what he has said or describing what she has done. You might say, "This is what I hear you saying . . . " Repeat or rephrase what the person has just said to you. Quite often, they'll feel understood and gratified that someone else can articulate what they are feeling or thinking.

Sometimes, however, the person may respond, "No, that's not it at all." At that point, you can say, "Maybe I misunderstood. Explain it to me again if you don't mind." Be aware that the person may not be objective enough to see the reality in his own statements. Either way, mirroring can lead to further discussion and understanding.

5. Stay in control.

As the discussion progresses, be aware of your feelings of hurt, fear, confusion, guilt, and anger. Notice your body language. Are you slumping in the chair as the other person blames you for every problem the two of you ever had? Sit up! Are you averting your eyes because you're afraid of her condemnation and venomous looks? Be strong! Look her in the eye and speak the truth. Are you leaning forward, interrupting the other person and yelling? Calm down. Sit back. Apologize. And listen.

6. Accept appropriate responsibility.

We may have made the assumption that the other person is 100 percent to blame and we're faultless, but often we contributed in some way to the problem. For instance, Phil had bailed out his alcoholic brother a dozen times with financial help. Each time, he told himself that he was doing the noble and loving thing for his brother. Only later did he realize that his enabling had prevented his brother from experiencing the consequences of his irresponsible behavior.

When Phil met with his brother to explain why he wasn't going to write him any more checks, he said, "I've done you wrong. I've treated you like a child, and I apologize. Please forgive me. I promise, I won't do it again."

His brother was shocked and disappointed that the money pipeline had closed, but he couldn't argue with Phil's genuine repentance. Heroes need to apologize for rescuing people and preventing their growth. Field marshals need to apologize for controlling the lives of weak, dependent people. And turtles need to apologize for not standing up for truth. Repentance for each of them looks different, but it can change the nature of a relationship.

7. Don't expect instant repentance.

When we finally find the courage to speak the truth, we're foolish to think most people will immediately respond, "You're exactly right. I've hurt you, and I'm truly sorry. Please forgive me. How can I make it up to you?" It happens, but not very often.

More commonly, a person's first response is a fierce defensive reaction to being confronted, whether the specific issues are simple or complex, relatively mild or serious, short-term or long. Give the person time to reflect, pray, and think about a response and set another appointment to continue the conversation in a few days.

Now What? Keep Pursuing Authentic Love

At the end of the confrontation, our course of action depends on the other person's response. The next step is simple if she says, "You're a jerk! I never did anything wrong!" or in contrast, "I'm sorry. What can I do to rebuild trust in our relationship?"

Most responses, though, lie in between these extremes. He may agree he has hurt you, but he blames you for most of the problem. She may use self-pity to get you to feel sorry for her and to get you to back off. He may say he's willing to change, but after multiple confrontations, no change has happened. He still says, "You don't understand. I'm really trying. Give me one more chance." (Which is what you've done thirty-seven times before.) If you finally draw the line and set limits and expectations, he'll try to make you feel so much guilt—or you may feel it on your own—that you believe you should give in "just one more time."

Whatever the person's response may be, we need to forgive. Even if he doesn't ask for forgiveness, even if she'll hurt us again, even if we don't want to forgive, we still need to forgive. It is unilateral. We forgive because it honors the Lord and frees us from bitterness and the bondage of seeking revenge. No one said it's easy—it's not.

But don't be confused: Forgiving doesn't mean we have to give in to manipulation. It doesn't mean we have to blindly trust again. It doesn't mean the hurt is magically erased. Reconciliation is based on trust, and trust must be proven over time. Even if both parties want to reconcile, it doesn't happen instantly. The commitment to reconciliation can happen in a moment, but the building of understanding, respect, and trust is a long process. So be strong, be cautious, and be wise, but forgive.

When we confront and forgive, we probably won't do it perfectly, but we can be confident that we've taken a big step in our maturity. Even if the person is belligerent and manipulative, and even if she says she's willing to change but won't, we can recognize that we did all we could do. We took initiative, we spoke the truth in love, we forgave, and we offered to build a new relationship based on the strong foundation of mutual trust. If she refuses to take our offer, we can know we've done our best. In a situation just like this, a friend of mine was asked how he felt when his sister refused his offer of reconciliation. "Strong and sad," he said. "Strong and sad."

Be aware that after a confrontation, we're especially vulnerable to the elation of success or the disappointment of failure. In either case, we tend to let our guard down and are at risk for sliding back into a familiar rut in the relationship. We may let the person treat us in the same old ways without confronting him. We may see a flash of change, and we're so excited we think, *It's all over! She'll never treat me that way again!*—and then feel devastated when she slips into the same pattern of manipulation as before. He may want to reconcile, but now the problem is us—we refuse to give an inch! Or perhaps the confrontation has taken all the punch out of us. We may feel emotionally empty, discouraged, and depressed.

We must remember that for years we've taught others how to treat us. When we cowered under their condemnation, we taught them that it was perfectly acceptable to talk to us like disobedient children. When we enabled them by fixing their problems, we taught them that they didn't ever have to be responsible—we might fuss and fume, but we'd take care of everything for them. And when we hid from meaningful interaction and conflict, we taught them that we didn't care about the relationship. Now, as we stand up, sit down, speak out, or shut up, we're teaching them a different lesson: we're going to behave like adults and learn what it means to truly love one another no matter what.

It may take quite some time for others to learn this new lesson. When we extend our hand and offer the opportunity for a healthy relationship, some will take it, but many won't. No matter how they respond, we remain tenaciously committed to honesty, wisdom, and strength. We continue to treat them with respect, speaking the truth and offering our hand— unless, of course, they bite it off.

After Phil confronted his mother and brother and offered them a new kind of relationship, they both turned him down— viciously, painfully, and completely. He continued to relate to both of them, but more guarded and with far lower expectations than before. "My door is always open," he told them. "If you ever want to have a real relationship, let me know." He had been foolish in the past, but no longer. When they tried to manipulate him, he sometimes confronted them, but more often, he simply didn't respond. He wasn't going to play their game, and he became so healthy that he didn't overreact. Today, he says, "I'd sure like to have a terrific relationship with my mom and my brother, but so far, it's not happening. Maybe someday. We'll see."

Those relationships haven't worked out like Phil hoped, but he has a far richer relationship with his wife and kids than ever.

"Would I go through it all again?" he reflects. "You bet. It was really hard, but it's taught me more than I could ever imagine. When I was a kid, I was terrified of my mother. Today, my children call me 'just to talk.' You have no idea what that means to me. It's one of the greatest gifts of God's grace in my life."

THINK ABOUT IT . . .

1. As you become a healthier, wiser, more responsible adult, in what ways might your family members (or whomever you're enmeshed with) feel threatened by the change? Explain your answer.

2. How have they tried to manipulate you and intimidate you to go back to the way things used to be? Has it worked in the past? Will it work now? Why or why not?

3. What are the possible benefits and risks of confrontation, and how committed are you to confronting when necessary?

4. Look over the list of principles for confrontation. Which ones look like they'll be fairly easy to accomplish? Which ones look more difficult? Who can help you to prepare?

5. What are some strategies to help you maintain self-control in the meeting, especially when the person pushes back?

6. In what ways have you taught people around you how they should treat you? In what ways are you retraining them now?

CHAPTER 13

SQUARE OFF
AGAINST EVIL

WHEN WE FORGIVE EVIL WE DO NOT EXCUSE IT,
WE DO NOT TOLERATE IT, WE DO NOT SMOTHER
IT. WE LOOK THE EVIL FULL IN THE FACE, CALL IT
WHAT IT IS, LET ITS HORROR SHOCK AND STUN AND
ENRAGE US, AND ONLY THEN DO WE FORGIVE IT.

—*Lewis B. Smedes*

In every human heart, God has put an instinctive sense of justice. Deep in our souls, we know what's right and wrong. We intuitively know that honesty is essential. We're outraged when evil prevails and are devastated when we are victims of injustice.

We may sense that healing and hope come only when we have the courage to expose our wounds to the light of God's truth and love. And that is true. However, the urge to keep our sins and hurts buried is powerful. We may hide behind layers of self-protection because:

- We think we'll come apart at the seams if we let our pain surface.

- We feel a profound and abiding sense of shame for what happened.

- We blame ourselves for what happened.

- We feel a need to exercise some measure of control.

- We have a strong sense of identity in being "the victim."

- We really don't think there's any hope of resolution, and hiding is the best we can imagine.

- We're afraid that other people—especially the ones who have hurt us—will use our awareness of the pain to hurt us again.

Whether we have been treated unjustly or have initiated the injustice, we may think that locking painful emotions in a box is a good solution. Unfortunately, we fail to see how much those unresolved hurts truly affect us. The poison leaks out, harming every relationship, every motive, and every choice. The consequences of avoiding reality can be devastating.

Consider what happened after King David's daughter, Tamar, was raped by her half-brother Amnon. She isolated herself from everyone around her (2 Samuel 13–19). David was furious, but did nothing. The denial and unresolved pain eventually erupted within the family—as it so often does—when Tamar's brother Absalom vengefully murdered Amnon and led Israel to rebel against David.

The more we harbor unresolved wounds and unconfessed sins, the more we'll hurt those we try to love.

Many of us live with a kind of moral schizophrenia: We condemn ourselves with vicious words of self-loathing, and blame others at the drop of a hat. At the same time, we deny there's anything wrong with our hearts.

The enmeshment that follows often compels us to recreate those family dynamics in other relationships. It is as if we seek to reset the "scene" at the point of trauma in the mistaken belief that we will somehow receive the happy ending—the love, the affirmation, the safety or protection—we so desperately needed way back then. Yet no matter how many times we go through the cycle, we never experience true freedom. Why? Because overcoming the impact of past wounds requires facing the truth.

Truth isn't some random choice. Neither is denial. Rather, denial is a strategy for self-preservation. Children who are victims of abuse typically can't face the reality that the perpetrator isn't safe, so they instinctively blame themselves for their abuser's sins. They don't feel safe enough to point their little fingers and say, "Look what you're doing to me. It's not right." So they soak up the blame and convince themselves that they deserve to be treated as they are. And of course, their abusers are quite happy to pass along the blame, which doubles the child's sense of shame and helplessness.

Adults, too, sometimes deny what's happened to create an illusion of safety or to minimize and cover up deeply rooted pain. When Bethany discovered her husband's porn addiction and years of deception, she instantly concluded, "It must be my fault. If I had been a better wife, and if I were prettier, he wouldn't look somewhere else."

Facing the Truth of Our Pain

Any family that fails to listen well and/or help its members process pain produces an unsafe environment where unresolved anger and ungrieved hurt intensify until they become overwhelming. In disruptive homes, it's not only children who cover up the hurt, anger, and fear. Everyone is affected.

People who grow up in chaotic, pain-filled families may spend their waking hours masking hurt and numbing anger, but they are often consumed by fear.

The first step toward resolving the damage of injustice is to be completely honest about it. We may have excused the sin and/or the perpetrator in the past, and we may have tried to minimize the damage, but not anymore. Evil cannot be *extinguished* until and unless it can first be *distinguished*.

Some of us shrink back from this step because we're convinced God is a loving God who overlooks people's sins. But we dare not miss the fact that Scripture describes God as both loving *and* just. If we downplay his justice, we have a weak God who can't be trusted. Theologian Miroslav Volf, who endured mistreatment during the cruel Balkan Wars, writes about the necessity of understanding God's passion for justice: "If God were not angry at injustice and deception and did not make a final end to violence—that God would not be worthy of worship." He goes on to say that the lack of belief in a God who loves justice "secretly nourishes violence."[1]

Others of us shrink back because we think hurt, fear, and anger are less-than-Christian emotions. However, Jesus wasn't the "stained-glass guy" in the church window. He was perfect, but not stoic. His emotions ran the entire spectrum. He expressed outrage at the businessmen who turned the temple into a shopping center. He confronted the Pharisees. He wept at the tomb of Lazarus. He was joyful at the good report after sending out the seventy.

God is no stranger to the emotions we feel in response to injustice. He is no stranger to our pain. When his heartache over injustice almost overwhelmed him, the psalmist Asaph wanted to scream, "It's not fair!"

Listen to his heart. Notice the depth of his despair and the moment God gave him insight:

> When my heart was grieved
>   and my spirit embittered,
> I was senseless and ignorant;
>   I was a brute beast before you.
> Yet I am always with you;
>   you hold me by my right hand.
> (Psalm 73:21–23)

God is right with us in our pain. He is "a great high priest who has passed through the heavens, Jesus the Son of God. . . . one who has been tempted in all things as we are, yet without sin. Therefore let us draw near with confidence to the throne of grace so that we may receive mercy and find grace to help in time of need" (Hebrews 4:14–16 NASB).

Learning to Forgive

C. S. Lewis once remarked, "Everyone says forgiveness is a lovely idea, until they have something to forgive."[2] Though forgiveness is at the heart of the Christian faith, sadly, many of us don't practice it very well. It remains a doctrine, an ideal we sing about, but it seldom touches us at the deepest level.

In order to heal from the power and pain of injustice, we must forgive—that is, "release someone from a debt." In order to forgive, we must first identify the loss we've experienced. It would seem to be an easy task (and for some, it is)—except that many of us have redefined reality for so long that we can't clearly articulate the injustices we've suffered.

When Nicole left her abusive boyfriend, for example, she and her newborn daughter moved half a continent away. In a safe environment with friends who loved her, she made halting progress in identifying the abuse she had suffered. Gradually, though, she began to replace her thoughts of excusing him with an honest appraisal of her wounds. When the full truth of the abuse hit her, she became furious. Her friends understood that her anger was valid; it was absolutely the right response to the injustice she had endured. But it wasn't until that point that she could begin to grieve and inch toward forgiveness.

Like Nicole, many of us need a safe place, some assistance, and plenty of time to let our defenses down so that we can be honest about the cold, hard facts of our lives. *Then* we can begin to grieve our losses. *Then* we can forgive the inexcusable in others, just as Jesus has done for us. The good news is that forgiveness doesn't require the permission or participation of the offending party. It's between God and us.

What about Payback?

Even when we're honest about our injury and committed to forgiveness, revenge will still occasionally tug at our hearts. That's why Philip Yancey called forgiving offenders "the unnatural act"—because it flies in the face of our desire for revenge.[3] And for some of us, revenge is our top priority:

> A man was bitten by a dog that was later discovered to have rabies. The man was rushed to the hospital, where tests showed that he, too, had contracted the highly contagious disease. At that time, medical science had not discovered a cure for rabies, so the doctor told the man he needed to get his affairs in order. The dying man sank back in his bed in shock for a few minutes, and then summoned the strength to ask for a pen and

paper. When the doctor stopped by a bit later to check on him, he was writing with great energy. The doctor said, "Oh, good. I'm glad to see you are working on your will."

"This ain't no will," the man answered. "It's a list of all the people I'm going to bite before I die!"[4]

Perhaps the reason we don't hear many sermons on revenge is because we could preach them ourselves! Forgiveness is not natural—it is *super*natural. The ability to forgive requires the grace of God flowing in and through us. Thankfully, God's grace has no limits.

Without Limits

When we examine the life of Jesus, we see that he forgave anyone who was willing to accept his gracious offer—prostitutes, the hated tax collector Zacchaeus, an outcast Samaritan woman, and even the soldiers who nailed him to the cross. His forgiveness knew no bounds, and he taught that there are no limits to forgiveness for those who are in God's kingdom.

To demonstrate limitless forgiveness, he told a parable about two servants in a king's court (Matthew 18:23–34). The first servant's debt to the king was ten thousand talents. A *talent* was a measure of precious metal (about seventy pounds of gold or silver). Some Bible scholars have noted that this amount of money was equal to the gross domestic product of the three surrounding nations. The point was that the debt was so astronomical that it was impossible to repay.

The servant was brought before the king and repayment was demanded, but of course, he didn't have enough money. The king ordered him to be thrown into debtors' prison, but the man pleaded for time to repay his debt. The king reneged and completely forgave his debt. This man had come before the throne with an incredible debt, no hope for repaying it, and a looming life sentence. He walked out completely free!

Yet as the servant left the palace, he saw a fellow servant who owed him a few dollars. He not only demanded to be repaid right then and there, but he grabbed the man and choked him! The second servant pleaded for time to pay back what he owed, but the first servant refused, ordering that the man be thrown into debtors' prison until the full amount was paid.

When the king heard what had happened, he was outraged. He called the servant back into the palace and said, "You wicked servant. I canceled all that debt of yours because you begged me to. Shouldn't you have had mercy on your fellow servant just as I had on you?"

The king imprisoned the man until he paid back the full amount of his original debt. At the end of the parable, Jesus utters one of the most piercing statements in the Bible: "This is how my heavenly Father will treat each of you unless you forgive your brother from your heart" (Matthew 18:35 NIV1984).

The first servant in Jesus' story represents us. Our debt of sin to our King is so enormous that we have no way to repay it. Our only hope is to fall on his mercy and beg for forgiveness.

Those who truly appreciate the depth of God's grace are eager to share God's gift of forgiveness with others. Those whose hearts aren't filled with grace and gratitude act like the first servant in the story: they refuse to forgive those who have hurt them, wanting to choke the life out of them instead.

God isn't happy when his children fail to follow his example of generous forgiveness. If we refuse to pass along the forgiveness God has poured out on us, he permits us to be tormented by bitterness, self-pity, regret, and thoughts of revenge. These are choking weeds in the garden of our hearts—weeds that will ruin our relationships and block the flow of the Spirit. Our refusal to forgive is a powerful hindrance to a life of freedom and joy.

Forgiveness Sets Us Free to Heal

When we forgive, we are set free from the destructive power of past events. In fact, our perception of those events changes. In *The Art of Forgiving*, author Lewis B. Smedes observes, "Forgiving does not erase the bitter past. A healed memory is not a deleted memory. Instead, forgiving what we cannot forget creates a new way to remember. We change the memory of our past into a hope for our future."[5]

The impact of the anger and bitterness that flows out of a wounded heart is a bit like grabbing hold of a wire with a strong electrical current running through it. While everything inside you screams to let go, the muscles in your hand involuntarily clamp the wire. You can't let go until someone cuts the power at its source. And although you will still suffer some degree of pain from your wounds, you can at least tend to the injury and allow the healing process to begin.

In a similar way, the act of forgiveness cuts the power and influence of our wounded past. Once we let go of what had literally gripped our souls, the Spirit of God can begin to heal and restore us.

When we refuse to forgive, we remain shackled to our old perceptions of the event. Our lack of forgiveness imprisons us in a life of resentment. We can come up with many reasons to refuse to forgive those who offend us:

- "He isn't sorry for what he did."
- "It wasn't an accident. He meant it!"
- "She hurt me again and again and again."
- "It was so horrible. How can I forgive something like that?"
- "She'll just do it again, so why bother?"
- "I can't forgive because I'm still so hurt and angry. I'd be a hypocrite."
- "It just doesn't make sense to let the offender off the hook. It's not fair!"
- "If I forgive, the person won't be brought to justice."

Yet by refusing to forgive, *we* remain victims and never make real progress toward healing.

If you want to heal, try heeding the apostle Paul's instruction: "Get rid of all bitterness, rage and anger, brawling and slander, along with every form of malice. Be kind and compassionate to one another, forgiving each other, just as in Christ God forgave you" (Ephesians 4:31–32).

Pat and I (Tim) recognize that forgiveness is unique to each of us and our situations. Sometimes, God grants the ability to forgive instantly. But most of the time, it takes longer—hours to days to months. There simply are no absolute formulas—emotions aren't tame creatures we can easily command.

The process of healing deep wounds requires patience. As you commit to walking the winding path of forgiveness, your heart will begin to heal. The powerful and painful feelings may never completely go away, but they will subside. You may live with a scar, but a scar is a sign of healing. As you heal, you will have more love to give.

REACH Forgiveness

Noted foregiveness expert Everett Worthington Jr. offers a practical model to REACH forgiveness:

Recall the hurt. This is difficult but necessary.

Empathize with the person who hurt you. Write a letter as if you were the one who hurt you. Communicate your thoughts, feelings, insights and pressures. Then write a letter of apology as if you were the person who hurt you. How difficult is it to do this?

Altruistic gift of forgiveness. Promote the "giving" of forgiveness. Think of a time when you hurt someone else and were forgiven. Reflect on the wrongdoing and guilt. How did it feel to be afforded mercy? Would you like to give that gift of forgiveness to the person who hurt you?

Commit to forgive. Write a certificate or letter of forgiveness, but don't send it.

Hold on to forgiveness when doubts arise.[6]

....

Bypass the Shortcuts

Is it true that, to feel better about life, we just need to let go of all the hurt, fear, and anger? On the surface, this advice sounds good, but it only represents a first step. Deeply entrenched emotions and recurring thoughts have the psychological consistency of peanut butter—the effects can stick with us and may require significant time to digest.

We can't just open our hands, drop away years of heartache, resentment, and self-pity, and expect complete restoration. We can't and shouldn't "just get over it and move on." We have to do the hard work of being ruthlessly honest about the hurt that occurred, the depth of its damage, our negative coping strategies, and the resulting dysfunctional habits that ensnare our daily lives.

We've probably all heard some well-meaning preacher tell his flock that forgiveness is a decision. And he's right. But it's a decision that often requires intentional focus to become a reality in our lives. This is because forgiveness is both an event and a process. People who have experienced a lifetime of manipulation, disrespect, injustice, and mistreatment have suffered significant losses. In order to forgive and heal, they need plenty of time to grieve. God takes us through that process at our own pace and in his own way. We won't make much progress, though, if we don't have friends who will speak the truth and support us each step of the way.

Individuals often make one of two mistakes when they face the choice of forgiving someone who hurt them: they forgive flippantly—telling themselves, "It was no big deal"—or they hold onto the hurt.

Flippant forgivers want to get over the feeling as fast as they can and usually try to avoid having a conversation with the offending person. Excusing and minimizing, though, isn't the same as forgiving; it's the path of avoidance.

Other people forgive too late or not at all. They harbor resentment for years, never realizing that by dwelling on the offender almost every day, or replaying the event again and again, they are anything but free. They may insist, "It's not hurting me!" but in reality, the bitterness is eating them alive.

From Forgiveness to Trust

When Phil's eyes were first opened to the craziness of his family, he had been a Christian for several years, and he knew he needed to forgive his father, his brother, and especially his mother. Yet he refused. He was certain that if he forgave them, he'd have to trust them, and he wasn't willing to jump into that boat again!

While God's command to forgive is unilateral, trust is an earned commodity. We are to forgive whether or not the other person confesses their fault.

Jesus told his disciples about something that can help us know when it is safe to move from forgiveness to trust: "I am sending you out like sheep among wolves. Therefore be as shrewd as snakes and as innocent as doves. Be on your guard" (Matthew 10:16–17).

God doesn't insist that we trust someone who is unwilling to take a step toward us, who isn't sorry for his or her part in the problem, and who blames us for the rift in the relationship. It would be foolish to trust someone like that. Reconciliation and trust require the other person to prove he is trustworthy.

Once Phil understood the difference between trust and forgiveness, he was able to let go of his bitterness toward his family. Now he could be free from the haunting thoughts and resentful feelings. Now he could offer his family a path toward a healthy, meaningful relationship.

When Phil talked to his dad and told him he was forgiven, his father wept. For the first time since Phil was a boy, they hugged and told each other, "I love you." It was a good beginning, but it was only the first step.

With a heart full of hope, Phil met with his brother and offered him a relationship based on trust and respect. His brother insisted, "I don't know what you're talking about; I never did anything to you," and then called Phil a number of nasty names and stormed out the door. Phil was deeply disappointed, but not shattered, because he had prepared for several possible responses.

Next, the hardest one of all: his mother. When Phil talked to his mom, he recounted a number of painful moments in their relationship. He told his mother that he forgave her, and she exploded, "You are so ungrateful! After all I've done for you all these years . . . and this is what you have to say to me?"

Phil responded with quiet strength, although he was shaking inside. "I would like to have a relationship of honesty and respect. We have a long way to go to rebuild trust."

His mother erupted again and blamed him for their family's problems. Phil was ready. Although he had dreaded this moment for a long time, he replied in a measured tone, "I don't agree with you, Mom. If you want to talk about our relationship in the future, let me know."

We can't make people become trustworthy. We can only be honest, forgiving, and strong—and offer a relationship based on mutual trust and respect. Some folks, like Phil's dad, will take us up on our offer and accompany us down the path toward rebuilt trust. Others, however, aren't—and may never be—willing to take those steps. If they reject our offer, we have another offense to forgive and another wound to grieve.

Choosing to Live in Truth

We live in a fallen world. People wound us and disappoint us, but our own foolish and sinful choices cause much of the pain we experience. When we're like Jesus, we weep over death, disease, divorce, and many other wounds in our lives and the lives of those we love. And because of Jesus, we know there's true hope for healing and change.

In his book *The Healing Path*, psychologist Dan Allender describes the spiritual perspective that can be ours when it comes to painful events in our lives:

> If we fail to anticipate thoughtfully how we will respond to the harm of living in a fallen world, the pain may be for naught. It will either numb or destroy us rather than refine and even bless us. . . . Healing in this life is not the resolution of our past; it is the use of our past to draw us into deeper relationship with God and His purposes for our lives.[7]

We can never really change other people . . . all we can change is ourselves. This process takes a lot of grace and strength that we don't have apart from God. But in his compassionate, creative hands, our wounds and sins can become the source of our deepest growth. They can become the platform from which we know when to stop giving in and when to push back against evil.

When we respond appropriately to our suffering, we have the opportunity to heal and experience true love in our most important relationships. We may not like the curriculum, but the classroom of suffering teaches us life's most important lessons and helps us make sense of our journey.

THINK ABOUT IT . . .

1. What kinds of injustice and evil are particularly painful to you?

2. What makes it so hard to face injustice, hurt, anger, and resentment in our lives?

3. What do Ephesians 4:31–32 and Romans 12:17–19 teach us about forgiveness? What steps do you need to take to apply them?

4. What are some differences between forgiveness and trust? Why is it important to understand they aren't the same thing?

5. How do we know when to trust someone who has repeatedly hurt us?

6. Facing our deepest pain and sins is a tough curriculum. What lessons do you think God wants to teach you as you square off against evil?

CHAPTER 14

WHEN THE WAY AHEAD IS DIFFICULT

COURAGE IS NOT THE ABSENCE OF FEAR, BUT
RATHER THE JUDGMENT THAT SOMETHING
ELSE IS MORE IMPORTANT THAN FEAR.

—Ambrose Redmoon

Two friends stood in line to order lunch at a fast-food restaurant. James ordered a salad. Mick gave him a look that said, "What's that about?" James replied, "I need to lose about five pounds."

"Me too," Mick told him, and then he told the guy behind the counter, "Give me a double cheeseburger and rings."

James smirked, "Is that the magic denial diet?"

Mick grinned, "Yep, that's the one. I plan to keep eating exactly what I've been eating and hope to lose the weight."

Too many of us follow Mick's strategy for emotional and

relational progress. We see a need to change, but we aren't willing to do the hard work to make it happen. Even with the best of intentions, we often fail to understand how hard it is to change decades of habits.

Virtually every person trying to grow up as an adult has hit the wall in their progress and wanted to quit. It's almost a given. After a month or two of hard work, they've gained some insight about their problems, but they've secretly hoped their attendance in counseling sessions or group meetings would make them feel better right away. They're shocked when they feel worse! They've uncovered long-buried hurts and resentment, and now, they realize, they have more to overcome than they ever dreamed.

At this point, many people bail out. They didn't sign on for more pain, more confusion, and a longer process. It's easier just to keep the peace. They expected to be fixed and happy by now!

When people get to this critical point, they need to understand that they aren't going crazy and their situation isn't hopeless. Now is not the time for wishful thinking. They must find the inner strength to keep pushing back against the resistance they face. They need to understand that you have to clean out the infection before healing can begin. And they have to know what steps to take to continue moving forward.

Don't Do It Alone!

In past relationships, we absorbed the messages (verbal and nonverbal) that said, "You'll never make it," "You'd better make me happy or else," or "You don't matter to me at all." Now we need to find new relationships that will encourage us to forge ahead on the right path. A few friends who are ruthlessly honest about their own lives will make a huge difference. As we watch them choose to live in truth, we'll be more willing to listen as they "truth" us by telling us what they see in our lives.

In the past, when we looked at the scowls on the faces of the people whose opinion of us we valued, we became defensive, depressed, or defiant. But now, convinced that our new friends truly love us, we begin to take down our protective walls and listen to what they say. We feel understood; deep in our souls, we believe we're known and loved for who we are. We don't have to wear masks any longer. Our new friends don't condemn us for our failures and they don't fix us. They respect us as adults.

We can also lean on our relationship with God to provide the wisdom, strength, and hope we need. At the end of one of the most powerful and beautiful chapters in the Bible, the prophet Isaiah reminds the people that God is supremely trustworthy. We may not understand what's going on around us or what God is doing behind the scenes, but we can trust in his wisdom, power, and love no matter what.

[The Lord] gives strength to the weary
>   and increases the power of the weak.
> Even youths grow tired and weary,
>   and young men stumble and fall;
> but those who hope in the LORD
>   will renew their strength.
> They will soar on wings like eagles;
>   they will run and not grow weary,
>   they will walk and not be faint.
> (Isaiah 40:29–31)

Along the way, God gives us flashes of insights to encourage us, but we all face times when we feel like giving up. When doubts weaken us and disappointments threaten to crush us, it takes all our strength to put one foot in front of the other. During such times we, like King David, can trust that God will give clear guidance in the darkness.

> I remain confident of this:
>   I will see the goodness of the LORD
>   in the land of the living.
> Wait for the LORD;
>   be strong and take heart
>   and wait for the LORD. (Psalm 27:13–14)

We may not see the end of our suffering yet, and we may not have all the answers to our questions, but we have the assurance that God is loving, strong, and wise. If we stay close to him, he'll give us the strength we need.

Waiting is a common theme in Scripture. It isn't primarily about time; it's about heart. We wait for God to work in us and through us, expecting him to reveal himself in his way and in his timing. We expect him to be faithful to his promises, but we remember that he isn't obligated to follow our schedule.

Waiting, however, doesn't mean we remain passive. As we look to God for wisdom, we continue to take bold steps to live in truth.

Clearly Identify the Love You Desire

We've taken a long look at how we can misunderstand the true nature of love. But to move forward, we need crystal-clear thinking. We need a benchmark in our minds of where we've come from and where we need to go. We need to write a statement of what we believe true love is . . . what love looks like, feels like, tastes like, and smells like . . . that clarifies what we've lost and what we want.

Like a creative writing project in high school or college, we write, edit, and proof our work, and then work on it again. When we're ready, we can read it to our most trusted friends to get their feedback. When we're done, we have a powerful statement that we can come back to again and again when our thinking gets fuzzy.

When Kim did her homework to clarify her concept of love, she quickly jotted down the ways her relationship with Jasper was based on intimidation and compliance. For days, she wrote and rewrote her statement, and finally she read it to her counselor:

> I've been wrong about love. I thought it was loving for me to give in to my husband's demands, but it only gave him permission to control me more. If I love him, I'll act like an adult, speak the truth, and stand up to his intimidation. I'll offer him a real relationship and see what happens. But being an adult also means that I don't give in to bitterness and fear. I choose to forgive—as many times as necessary—as I grow stronger, trusting in God's love, justice, and strength.

Kim's statement may not win a literary award, but it was golden. She memorized it, and the sentiments gave her perspective and direction in tough times between her and Jasper.

Fill Your Mind with Truth and Hope

Our oppressive thoughts, as well as our manipulative habits, are like old computer software. No matter how much we want to get different results, we'll stay stuck in the same pattern until we install a new program. Changing the way we think is possible, but it takes concerted effort.

Paul compared this process to siege warfare. In his second letter to the Corinthians, he wrote, "For though we live in the world, we do not wage war as the world does. The weapons we fight with are not the weapons of the world. On the contrary, they have divine power to demolish strongholds. We demolish arguments and every pretension that sets itself up against the knowledge of God, and we take captive every thought to make it obedient to Christ" (2 Corinthians 10:3–5).

Our old thought processes are "strongholds" that have to be "demolished" in a concerted, disciplined, consistent battle between our ears. Like an army gathering resources to besiege a city, we find books, groups, friends, quotes, and passages of Scripture as our battle supplies. In the fight, we realize we've had wrong thoughts about God ("arguments and pretensions" in Paul's terminology). We may have thought that God doesn't love us; if he did, he'd change difficult people so they're nice to us, or he'd take us out of the situation completely so we wouldn't hurt any longer.

As we grow into strong adults, our thinking matures, and we understand that God's purpose is often quite different than ours: in every situation, he wants us to trust him, grow strong and wise, and respond to present realities with bold love. That is the truth. That is our hope.

In strained relationships, it's easy to lose hope. We try hard to control the other person's behavior, but it just doesn't work . . . at least, it doesn't work as well as we'd like. Soon, confusion turns to disappointment, and disappointment morphs into deep discouragement. We believe we're total failures and God has let us down.

Walter Ciszek knew something about disappointment. Ciszek felt led by God to be a minister in Russia, but the church sent him instead to Poland. When the Nazis invaded Poland in 1939 and the borders with Russia suddenly opened, Ciszek thought his prayers were answered. He slipped across the border, but he was soon captured as a spy and sent to a Soviet prison. He suffered for five years in solitary confinement, then for many more years in a harsh gulag. During that time, God worked deeply in Ciszek's heart. He was tempted to be resentful and wallow in self-pity, but God gave him patience and wisdom. In his book, *He Leadeth Me*, Ciszek reflected,

> Each day to me should be more than an obstacle to be gotten over, a span of time to be endured, a sequence of hours to be survived. For me, each day came forth from the hand of God newly created and alive with opportunities to do his will. . . . We for our part can accept and offer back to God every prayer, work, and suffering of the day, no matter how insignificant or unspectac-

ular they may seem to us. . . . Between God and the individual soul, however, there are no insignificant moments; this is the mystery of divine providence.[1]

Step Back for a Clearer View

The people whose stories we've told were too close to see clearly in the early stages of dealing with their pain and problems. When they were able to step back from their most difficult relationships, they were able to see them with fresh eyes. Then they could think more clearly, process their repressed or explosive feelings, and make good choices about what they needed to do.

Quite often, when an enmeshed person is asked, "What are your options?" she replies with a look of confusion and says, "What do you mean, options? There's only one thing to do, and it's what I've always done."

The inability to identify multiple options can be one of the biggest hurdles on the path of real progress. Many people remain stuck for years because they can't imagine any other way to live. They struggle, they suffer, and they complain, but they never take a step to change things. In Al Anon, a love for the familiar is clearly identified as strangely attractive and powerfully enslaving. The old saying goes: "It may be hell, but at least I know the names of the streets."

We can't learn to think and act differently in constant proximity to a manipulative person. We must get far enough away for a long enough time to see what we face and come up with a good plan of action. How far is far enough? For some, it's a drive to a support group or for coffee with an understanding friend. For others, the distance may need to be measured in hundreds or thousands of miles. How long is long enough? It may take only a walk outside, or an extended separation from the enmeshed person. To figure out what you need, talk to your counselor, pastor, or group leader.

The principle of stepping back for a clearer view works when we face a crisis too. When we're too close, a crisis looks like the end of the world. When Nicole's home pregnancy test showed she was pregnant, she was devastated. She was a teenager in a relationship with an abusive boyfriend. She thought, *My life is over. What am I going to do?* She didn't realize that the greatest crisis of her life offered an opportunity for growth, change, and maturity.

Today, with the distance of time on her side, she looks back on that time and wonders, *Who was that scared, intimidated girl?* God used the child growing inside her to get her attention and give her a new direction. When she looked at the plus sign on the test that day, she had no idea that a few years later she'd be free from her abusive boyfriend, happily married with three children, and a light in the darkness for troubled young women.

Crises seem utterly cataclysmic. The heartache and darkness of a crisis can be overwhelming, but God is the master of turning mourning into dancing and darkness into light. If we step back, we might catch a glimpse of what he sees.

In Romans, Paul points out how God uses our suffering to stimulate our faith and shape our lives: "We also glory in our sufferings, because we know that suffering produces perseverance; perseverance, character; and character, hope. And hope does not put us to shame, because God's love has been poured out into our hearts through the Holy Spirit, who has been given to us" (Romans 5:3–5).

God will use even our most difficult moments to produce the qualities of Jesus in us as we trust him. And he'll replace our shame with hope—the assurance that our lives matter and God loves us dearly. We may not like the curriculum God has for us, but the outcome is sweet: hope and love.

Imagine a New Way to Live

Most people who read books about emotional healing, meet with counselors, and attend support groups understand the principles of being an adult who experiences true love in key relationships. But when they are asked, "What does it look like to respond like an adult to a difficult person?" they look dazed and confused.

In our pathology of enmeshment or isolation, we have used our imaginations in powerful—and sometimes destructive—ways: to envision escape, dramatic rescues, dominating others, even to relive the shame of past failures. Now we must learn to channel our thoughts in a more productive direction. Envisioning ourselves as wise, mature adults is essential if we are to take big steps forward. We need to study our new roles in the way an actor becomes consumed with his character.

In an insightful book on Paul's letter to the Ephesians, pastor and theologian Timothy Gombis observes that the message of this letter (and in fact, the entire Bible) is that God's truth can thoroughly transform the way we think about every aspect of life. He notes:

> Our imaginations are shaped by our fears, our hopes, our experiences, our family history, our friendships and the way that we were hurt or praised by authority figures in our lives, to name only a few significant factors. All of these things, and many more, go into shaping the way we conceive of the world and our place in it. . . . My imagination also informs how I behave toward others and sets before me a range of potential options for conduct in any situation. . . . The gospel calls us to put off destructive, oppressive, and idolatrous roles that we have adopted to this point in our lives and to enter the truth fully, taking on and inhabiting roles that are supplied to us by the gospel of Jesus Christ.[2]

The message of the Bible is that those who have accepted Christ's gracious offer are now God's dear children, more valuable than all the diamonds, oil, real estate, and other treasures of the earth—in fact, more precious to God than the stars in the sky. This truth thrills us and humbles us. It provides the security we've longed for and the direction we need to chart a new course for our lives. We no longer live to please, prove, and hide, but to honor the One who paid the ultimate price to prove his love for us.

How can our imaginations work for us? Waving a magic wand or praying a single prayer doesn't renew our minds. The truth of God's grace and power sinks deep into our thoughts as we meditate, reflect, ponder, and consider passages of Scripture—like Paul's letter to the Ephesians. But his truth truly transforms us when we find the courage to act out our new roles, to live like we believe we are treasured by God, to gain wisdom as we consider who and how to trust the people around us, and as we make choices to assume or decline responsibilities.

As our imaginations change, we become more insightful about the past, the present, and the future. The events and people who haunted our minds no longer threaten us because we now see that God used them—even *them!*—to draw us closer to him and give us reference points by which to live differently. Gombis encourages us, "I have a radically new and renewed set of tools with which to remember my past, allowing me—

inviting me, empowering me—to rethink all things in light of what God has done in Christ to renew my present and future."[3]

To renew her imagination, Nicole decided to read Paul's letter to the Ephesians four or five times. By the third time, she noticed key themes such as her identity in Christ, the depth of God's forgiveness, and his purpose for her life. She had taken drama classes in high school, so she studied those themes like an actor preparing for a leading role. She imagined herself as a loved, forgiven, strong, wise person in whom God delights, and she envisioned responding to the difficult people in her life with clarity, hope, and courage.

We don't have a thousand different scenarios that cause problems in our relationships. Most of us can easily identify a few recurring ones: believing a spouse's or a prodigal's lies, feeling abandoned, and acting like a hero, field marshal, or turtle. Nicole's counselor encouraged her to pick one of these, and write a description of what usually happens and her usual response. With practice, Nicole learned to envision herself as a stronger, emotionally healthier version of herself who trusts cautiously, asks good questions, and has clear boundaries of responsibility.

Every situation is somewhat unique, and every person's path has its own twists and turns. We have to find the inner strength to get on the road, but we don't have to figure it out by ourselves. Find a friend, and when you inevitably hit a road-block, keep going to find a way around it.

THINK ABOUT IT . . .

···

1. What are the evidences (reflected in words, attitudes, expectations, and disappointments) that someone thinks change should happen easily and quickly, almost by magic? How do those people respond to difficulties on the journey of healing and hope?

2. Why is it important to make a commitment to uncovering and living by truth?

3. Make a first attempt at writing your definition of love.

4. What are some ways you already are filling your mind with hope and truth? What are some additional resources to help you?

5. What are you doing to create a healthy distance from the difficult people and crises in your life so that you can see your options more clearly? In what ways does your perspective change when you allow yourself some distance?

6. Of the suggestions offered in this chapter, which ones are the highest priorities for you right now? Explain your answer.

CHAPTER 15

THE VIEW FROM TOMORROW

WE CANNOT CHANGE OUR PAST. WE CANNOT CHANGE THE FACT THAT PEOPLE ACT IN A CERTAIN WAY. WE CANNOT CHANGE THE INEVITABLE. THE ONLY THING WE CAN DO IS PLAY ON THE ONE STRING WE HAVE, AND THAT IS OUR ATTITUDE.

—*Charles R. Swindoll*

Life can be different.

For things to change, we have to dig deep to find the conviction to chart a new course. But remember, half measures won't do. Danish theologian and philosopher Søren Kierkegaard observed, "Life can only be understood backwards; but it must be lived forwards."[1] When we're in the middle of our struggles, we feel confused and anxious about the next obstacle we'll face. Occasionally, we know we're making good progress, but at other times, we wonder if it's worth all the pain and effort.

When we drive a twisting mountain highway, we have our eyes glued to every bend in the road. Others may look at the beautiful scenery, but we can't. We're trying to avoid a catastrophe! But when we get to the top of the mountain and get out of the car, we can look back into the valley and appreciate how far we've come. The whole road comes into view, and we realize we've made it.

When it comes to rewriting the story of our lives—to making the journey from enmeshment to healthy, loving relationships—many of us are still on the mountainside with our eyes fixed on the road. We're not sure what's around the bend in our relationships, and we aren't even sure this long road will take us to a new and improved version of ourselves: someone with a sense of identity, wisdom, clear limits of responsibility, and honest, loving connections with at least a few people. Others have told us the view from the summit is beautiful, though, and based on their assurances, we keep going.

As Bethany approached the summit, she looked back on her process of becoming mature. Her comments echo the sentiments of the others whose lives we've chronicled: "The last couple of years have been difficult but wonderfully liberating. I wouldn't give anything for the things I've learned and the new friends I've made. In many ways, I've come alive. I had no idea how much I was living in fear. Now, I can look forward to each day—not because I have all the answers, but because I'm not threatened by not having them."

The Curriculum Is Tough

When we're driving up the mountain, the road is not easy or smooth. We learn the most important truths by boldly facing deceit and denial. We gain courage by confronting our fears. We find out the meaning of love by recognizing the counterfeit of manipulation. These and all the other rich lessons we learn, though, are acquired in the school of hard knocks.

In *The Gulag Archipelago*—a gripping account of the Soviet prison system—Alexander Solzhenitsyn describes surprise arrests of innocent people, mock trials, cruel tortures, and long years in punishing camps across the country. But in one of those camps, a doctor told the young atheist Solzhenitsyn about Christ's love and forgiveness, and the moment changed his life forever. One of his stories from the camps was about a man who was finally released after years of suffering behind the barbed wire. When the gates were opened and he walked into freedom, he stopped, turned back, and kissed the concrete wall. He cried grateful tears because it was there, in all the horror and pain, that he found Christ, new life, and true hope.[2]

As we take the first steps toward truth and love, we long to be totally free and unencumbered by the past. Although we can experience the wonderful benefits of God's love, forgiveness, and purpose now, as long as we're walking this planet, we'll still struggle to some degree with old desires. Making progress isn't like a helicopter ride to the top of the mountain. It's much more like a long hike up steep trails. Sometimes we trudge for a long distance with our heads down and see only the next step in front of us. But occasionally, we round a corner and are met with a spectacular view. We realize we're making progress, and all the sweat and pain is worth it.

A now-divorced Bethany explained, "I've grown so much since those days when I believed Rick's accusations that it was my fault he was addicted to porn. I still have fleeting doubts: Could I have done something different? What if I had done this or that? But when I have those doubts, I soon realize he made his choices. I tried to fix him, and I couldn't do it. I had to let him own his choices and his consequences. I offered to work toward a real relationship, but he walked away from me."

People who are far up the mountain on their journey are still focused on the road, but they've already come a long, long way. They aren't as driven as they used to be. They don't enable, intimidate, or hide as much as they used to, and they've given their families and friends permission to tell them when they slip into past patterns of behavior. They're charting a new course for their lives and their loved ones. It's not perfect—there are still scars, urges, and doubts—but their lives are far better than they ever dreamed.

Progress always comes at a price. In his letter to the Ephesians, Paul says that the old, destructive way to live is characterized by faulty thinking, darkened understanding, ignorance, and hard hearts. In contrast, believers are in a new school. He explains that the previous, destructive pattern of thought and behavior "is not the way of life you learned when you heard about Christ and were taught in him in accordance with the truth that is in Jesus" (Ephesians 4:20–21). In other words, we go to Christ's school to learn how to live. His instructions come with classes, tests, tutors, and an internship program so we can learn to put our new wisdom into practice.

What is the syllabus? Paul tells us, "You were taught, with regard to your former way of life, to put off your old self, which is being corrupted by its deceitful desires; to be made new in the attitude of your minds; and to put on the new self, created to be like God in true righteousness and holiness" (Ephesians 4:22–24).

Christ is the most accomplished teacher the world has ever known, and his tests are tough. As we make daily choices to "put off" our old, destructive habits, we can then "put on" new choices, which become new habits once our minds are renewed by our times in God's Word.

We're writing a new story for our lives. In the past, we let others hold the pen, but no longer. Now we pick it up and begin drafting a new plot . . . full of courage, love, and meaning. Of course, there are twists in the story, but we're not overwhelmed by fear any longer.

Writing a New Story

We may describe the rewriting of our stories in different ways. People have called it, "breaking the curse," "installing new relational software," or "unhooking from the past and making new connections in the future." All of us, though, are changing the plot and creating a different heritage for ourselves and the people we care about. As we set out on our journey, we realize that some of the people we love don't want to go with us, but we're unwilling to remain stuck in the mud any longer. We'll treat them with respect, love, and honesty, but we're committed to creating a happier, healthier future for our children and loved ones.

When Phil was in the middle of his climb out of his tangled relationships with his father, mother, and brother, he was fiercely determined to break the generational pattern he saw when he looked back at both sides of his parents' families. His daughter Tammy was eight years old, but he wanted to start making changes immediately. He sat down with her and explained, in an age-appropriate way, how his family had affected him when he was growing up. He talked about anger, manipulation, and fear.

Tammy wasn't surprised. Even as a little girl, she had seen enough of these forces at work when they visited her grandparents. Phil told her, "Honey, I've treated you that way too, and I want you to know that I'm very sorry. Will you forgive me?"

She nodded and smiled.

Then Phil said, "Tammy, here's the deal. I'm making a commitment to treat you with respect and love. Whenever you feel that I'm using anger or demands to control you, I want you to let me know."

Tammy grinned, "Does that mean I don't have to do what you tell me to do?"

Phil laughed, "No, it sure doesn't. But it means you can ask me about anything I tell you to do, and I promise I'll listen. You'll probably still need to do it, but at least you'll feel understood and valued."

Tammy agreed, and a few days later, she told her dad that she felt he was using a condemning tone when he told her to clean up her room. Phil melted, "You're right. I'm so sorry. Thanks for telling me. I'd like to say it won't happen again."

"I know it will," Tammy smiled at her dad. "But you're trying, Daddy. That's good."

These conversations began a radical transformation in Phil's family. He and his wife began talking about things they had buried years ago, and they learned to resolve current problems. Instead of seeing each other as adversaries fighting for control, they were allies in reshaping their family story. It was a beautiful thing to see.

When We Face Dead Ends

Of course, not all of our days will be beautiful; not all of our relationships will have happy endings. We can't control others' responses to our progress. We can only invite them to come with us. Some will . . . some won't.

When we get frustrated with baby steps, our more mature

friends can put their hands on our shoulders and assure us, "Don't worry. God is doing things you can't even see. Count on it." When we're not sure what's going on, we can be confident God knows. When we face dead ends, God is preparing to show us a different doorway. When we think we're alone and abandoned, God is right by our side.

In C. S. Lewis' *The Horse and His Boy*, Shasta is lost in a fog. He can't find the king's procession as he wanders blindly, but he has the feeling that he's not alone—something is near him in the darkness. He decides to talk to the stranger, and he tells his sad story of difficulties and struggles. He explains that twice, lions had chased him. In fact, he interpreted every appearance of lions as an ill omen. Shasta laments, "If nothing else, it was bad luck to meet so many lions."

The unseen companion announces that he is Aslan—the Christ-figure in Lewis' chronicles—the same lion Shasta has met during all his travels. Shasta is stunned by this revelation. Aslan continues,

> I was the lion who forced you to join with Aravis. I was the cat who comforted you among the houses of the dead. I was the lion who drove the jackals from you while you slept. I was the lion who gave the Horses the new strength of fear for the last mile so that you should reach King Lune in time. And I was the lion you do not remember who pushed the boat in which you lay, a child

near death, so that it came to shore where a man sat, wakeful at midnight, to receive you.[3]

When we feel alone, wondering where God could possibly be, we can know that he's as close as our breath, he loves us dearly, and he has our best interests at heart. Often, he doesn't rescue us out of our predicaments. Instead, his purpose is very different. He's not committed to our comfort, but to deepening our trust in him. His training always includes times of light and times of darkness, wonderful people who encourage us, and enough difficult people to drive us to prayer. Through it all, Christ—the Aslan of God—is actively and attentively accomplishing his sovereign, good purposes.

Our Privilege

Our life's stories aren't just for our benefit. As we experience God's love, power, and wisdom, he'll use us to provide comfort for those who are hurting and insight for those who are confused. Along the way, we have the incredible privilege of extending a helping hand to others who are on the journey. On Tim's and my path, God provided some people to help us at crucial moments, and now he puts us in others' lives to help them overcome the obstacles they face.

As we encounter people who are struggling in their most cherished relationships, our hearts break for them because we've been there, and we know what they're going through.

But we don't fix them, we don't smother them with directives, and we don't demand they obey our instructions. We act like Jesus, offering love and support with an open hand and a full heart, and we let others make their own choices about how and when to respond. We know that cutting God's curriculum short won't do the person any good. We've learned the most important lessons of our lives in the classroom of suffering, and we have no doubt that God wants to use it to teach our friends too. We become tutors, supporters, and cheerleaders as they learn.

As we make progress up the mountain, we feel a deep sense of gratitude that our lives are going in a new direction. There *is* a tomorrow . . . a *good* tomorrow. We can look back and see that we aren't stuck in the past any longer. We're gradually discovering the true meaning of love. Certainly, we still face a lot of challenges, but we have that wonderful, glorious commodity that makes life worthwhile: we have hope. We can step forward into uncertainty because we're confident that God loves us and is at work to fulfill his purposes in our lives. We're confident that the view from tomorrow is in his hands. When you are able to see and embrace this truth—there's your breakthrough!

THINK ABOUT IT . . .

1. Think of your favorite story, movie, novel, or biography. What is the test the central character faces, and what does the character exemplify by his or her response?

2. Does it encourage you or discourage you to know: "Life can only be understood backwards; but it must be lived forwards"? Explain your answer.

3. What kind of life story do you want to leave behind? What are some specific things you're doing today to change it for the better?

4. Have you seen your struggles as God's school to teach you how to live or as hindrances to your happiness? What's the difference in your response to each perception of your problems?

5. How do you think God will use you to help others who are struggling with their definition of love?

6. What are the most significant insights you've gained from this book?

7. What's your next step?

Break Through to Great Parenting

In chapter 9, we explored the need for parents to provide roots and wings for their kids. But what are other keys to great parenting?

Effective Parents Accept Changes in the Relationship

In a scene that has been reenacted hundreds of times, a couple went to a counselor for help with their fourteen-year-old daughter. Janice complained, "I don't know what happened to our sweet little girl. Tonya has always been so kind and loving; we've never had any problem with her before."

Her husband, Daniel, jumped in to explain, "It's so strange. Everything we've always liked, she now hates: music, television shows, movies, food, everything. I've always rooted for my college team, but now she cheers—right in front of me—for our archrival." He took a deep breath and asked, "I've read articles about oppositional defiant behavior. Is that what it is?"

The counselor knew their daughter well enough to suspect a very different diagnosis. Smiling at the distraught couple, he told them, "No, she's being a teenager. Tonya's hit that phase called adolescence, where the job of every young person is to carve out his or her own identity."

Psychologists call this *individuation*;[1] it's the process of an adolescent becoming a fully functioning individual instead of an extension of the parents. This doesn't mean that parenting no longer matters at this stage. Quite the contrary. It means that parents are parenting their children through a transition into adulthood. However, a common way for a child to take this step is to test and question whatever has been meaningful to the parents.

The counselor continued, "Not only is your daughter's behavior entirely normal, it's essential. In this respect, she's doing what all normal, healthy teenagers do. She's growing up, becoming a whole, healthy person who is independent of you. She's creating her own identity in the only way she knows how: by staking out differences from current expectations and authorities, which means she will naturally question the opinions, beliefs, values, interests, and tastes of those around her."

He paused to let this sink in and then explained, "You have two options—resist or celebrate. The road you choose will produce one of two different results: tremendous conflict and heartache, or remarkable growth and joy for all of you. Choose wisely."

Daniel and Janice were exhausted and confused. Like most parents at this juncture, they were inclined to impose additional rules rather than working on the relationship with their daughter. However, that pathway leads only to increased distance. On the other hand, rules combined with relationship lead to respect.

Fortunately, Daniel and Janice realized the wisdom of the counselor's observations.

They didn't have to take every disagreement with their daughter personally. They could let some less important things slide and learn how to open dialogue about the most significant issues, even when Tonya questioned their views. Over time, they realized that demanding instant compliance from Tonya had created some unnecessary tension and eroded their daily communication.

When Daniel and Janice chilled out and quit sweating so much of the small stuff, their relationship with Tonya improved. They laughed with their daughter instead of constantly correcting her. When Tonya wanted to paint her nails a horrid color, for example, her mom took her to the store and suggested some colors that were even more garish. They came to enjoy great conversations about all kinds of things, and began to build a new kind of relationship with her—one that would one day lead to them valuing each other as peers once she became an adult.

Effective Parents Weather Challenges to the Status Quo

With some parents, you'd think the goal of parenting during the teenage years was: "Control our kid's behavior so he (or she) doesn't embarrass us."

There's no question that teenagers need structure—roles, rules, and expectations. Imposing excessive rules on your teenager, or making all the decisions for them, may have the short-term benefit of controlling immediate behavior, but parents who persist in smothering and demanding behavior communicate, "I don't trust you, and I don't believe you're competent to make choices without me." This produces insecure, angry young men and women who aren't prepared to make it in the adult world. So one of the puzzles parents need to figure out is what's important and what's not. Not every issue is crucial. As the saying goes, you need to "Choose the hill you want to die on."

For example, seventeen-year-old Greg had matured remarkably since some major mess-ups academically and with friends his freshman and sophomore years of high school. Now as a senior, his parents had become his greatest fans instead of his constant critics. They had learned as much as he had during those tumultuous early years.

When basketball season started, however, Greg announced that he and the rest of the team were going to get Mohawk haircuts. Immediately, the tension level soared. His dad defiantly told him, "No, you're not!" His mom didn't want her friends to think she was a bad parent who let her son look like a clown, but she couldn't stand the thought of going back to the resentment and bickering that had plagued the family a few years earlier.

To help resolve the issue, Greg asked his dad to talk to a friend about the request, which he did. The friend simply asked, "What's the big deal? The hockey team bleached their hair blonde last year. It lasted a couple of months—and then, life resumed as normal!"

Greg's dad looked stunned. He wondered, *Why doesn't he think it's a big deal?*

The friend continued, "Look, hair grows out. This obviously means something to Greg. Instead of getting in his way, I'd offer to buy him a hair trimmer if I were you, so he could keep it neat all season."

Greg's dad hadn't considered helping his son with his crazy haircut, but he realized his friend was right. So he went home and told his son that he'd been wrong and that he would not object to the haircut. To no one's surprise, Greg hated the Mohawk after all. It lasted only a month.

Effective Parents Focus on the Future

Parenting to provide roots and wings is particularly important for children who come into adolescence with greater needs. The pastor of parents who were struggling with a teenager with attention deficit disorder wisely advised, "Your goal when he walks out the door—whether he's eighteen and going to college or getting a job and an apartment—is for him to feel confident about himself."

Do you know why? Because every kid needs at least one person who is crazy about them!

These parents had been focusing on all the things their son had been doing wrong. Their pastor's warning helped them to realize that their constant nagging had crushed their son's spirit. Immediately, they changed their game plan, and in only a matter of days, the atmosphere of the home radically changed. Their son wasn't suddenly more responsible and detailed, but because Mom and Dad had started focusing on what he did well, it relieved stress in their relationship, lowered the parents' blood pressure, and helped the son develop a more healthy self-esteem.

In this more supportive environment, their son began to change. A few years later, he left for college as a strong, confident young man. He graduated in five years, and today he has a meaningful job, a loving wife, and fun friends. His parents would say that the turning point came when their pastor told them to change their parenting goal. It made all the difference.

Whatever your specific goals for your son or daughter, make use of these overall principles. Refer to them often. They're valid for any kid—and any parent—as you together forge a family path toward a future of loving well.

How to Use This Book in Groups and Classes

This book is designed for individual study, small groups, and classes. The best way to absorb and apply these principles is for each person to individually study and answer the questions at the end of each chapter, then to discuss them in either a class or a group environment.

Each chapter's questions are designed to promote reflection, application, and discussion.

Order enough copies of the book for everyone to have a copy. For couples, encourage both to have their own book so they can record their individual reflections.

A recommended schedule might be:

Week 1   Introduction to the material. The group leader can tell his own story, share his hopes for the group, and provide books for each person. Encourage people to read the assigned chapter each week and answer the questions.

Weeks 2–15 Introduce the topic for the week and share a story of how God has used the principles in your life. In small groups, lead people through a discussion of the questions at the end of the chapters. In classes, teach the principles in each chapter, use personal illustrations, and invite discussion.

Personalize Each Lesson

Don't feel pressured to cover every question in your group discussions. Pick out three or four that had the biggest impact on you, and focus on those, or ask people in the group to share their responses to the questions that meant the most to them that week. Make sure you personalize the principles and applications. At least once in each group meeting, add your own story to illustrate a particular point.

Make the Scriptures come alive. Far too often, we read the Bible like it's a phone book, with little or no emotion. Paint a vivid picture for people. Provide insights about the context of people's encounters with God, and help people in your class or group sense the emotions of specific people in each scene.

Three Types of Questions

If you have led groups for a few years, you already understand the importance of using open questions to stimulate discussion. Three types of questions are *limiting*, *leading*, and *open*.

Many of the questions at the end of each lesson are open questions.

• *Limiting questions* focus on an obvious answer, such as, "What does Jesus call himself in John 10:11?" These don't stimulate reflection or discussion. If you want to use questions like this, follow them with thought-provoking open questions.

• *Leading questions* sometimes require the listener to guess what the leader has in mind, such as, "Why did Jesus use the metaphor of a shepherd in John 10?" (He was probably alluding to a passage in Ezekiel, but most people wouldn't know that.) The teacher who asks a leading question has a definite answer in mind. Instead of asking this question, he or she should teach the point and perhaps ask an open question about the point that's been made.

• *Open questions* usually don't have right or wrong answers. They stimulate thinking, and they are far less threatening because the person answering doesn't risk ridicule for being wrong. These questions often begin with "Why do you think ...?" or "What are some reasons that ...?" or "How would you have felt in that situation?"

Preparation

As you prepare to teach this material in a group or class, consider these steps:

   1. Carefully and thoughtfully read the book. Make notes; highlight key sections, quotes, or stories; and complete the reflection sections at the end of each chapter. This will familiarize you with the entire scope of the content.

2. As you prepare for each week's class or group, read the corresponding chapters again and make additional notes.

3. Adjust the amount of content to the time allotted. Pick the questions that are most pertinent, and if the conversation is rich, ask a follow-up question or two. It's important, though, to avoid getting bogged down. You may have to say, "We could talk a lot more about this question, but let's go on to the next one."

4. Add your own stories to personalize the message and add impact.

5. Before and during your preparation, ask God to give you wisdom, clarity, and power. Trust him to use your group to change people's lives.

6. Most people will get far more out of your meetings if they read the chapters and complete the reflection each week. Order books before the group or class begins or after the first week.

Notes

Chapter 1: In the Name of Love

1. Salvador Minuchin, *Psychosomatic Families: Anorexia Nervosa in Context* (Cambridge, Massachusetts: Harvard University Press, 1978), 30.

2. Sharon Wegshcheider-Cruse, *Choicemaking* (Pompano Beach, Florida: Health Communications Inc., 1987), 2.

3. Chart adapted from Tim Clinton & Gary Sibcy, *Attachments: Why You Love, Feel and Act the Way You Do* (Brentwood, Tennessee: Integrity Publishers, 2002), 50.

Chapter 2: Break Through to True Love

1. John Calvin, *Commentary on a Harmony of the Evangelists: Matthew, Mark, and Luke,* Matthew 5:38-41; Luke 6:29-30, Christian Classics Ethereal Library, http://www.ccel.org/ccel/calvin/calcom31.ix.xlix.html (accessed March 29, 2012).

2. Robert Hemfelt and Frank Minirth, *Love is a Choice* (Nashville, Tennessee: Thomas Nelson, 2003), 271.

3. N.T. Wright, *After You Believe: Why Christian Character Matters* (New York: HarperOne, 2010).

4. Laura Faidley, 2012.

5. You can read Stacy's story in Stacy Allison, *Beyond the Limits: A Woman's Triumph on Everest* (New York: Little Brown & Co, 1993); and *Many Mountains to Climb: Reflections on Competence, Courage and Commitment* (Bothell, WA: Hara Publishing, 1999)

6. Stacy Allison, "About Stacy," www.beyondthelimits.com, accessed May 18, 2011.

Chapter 3: Where's the Payoff?

1. Martin Seligman, *Authentic Happiness* (New York: Simon & Schuster, 2002).

Chapter 4: Answer the Wake-up Call

1. Elisabeth Elliot, *Keep a Quiet Heart* (Grand Rapids, Michigan: Revell, 2004), 38-39.

Chapter 5: Dismantling Our Idols

1. For a more complete review of how early caregiving relationships affect the brain function of an infant, see Allan N. Schore, "Effects of a Secure Attachment Relationship on Right Brain Development, Affect Regulation, and Infant Mental Health," *Infant Mental Health Journal,* 22, no. 1/2 (Jan.-April 2001), 7-66; "Hardwired to Connect: The New Scientific Case for Authoritative Communities, Executive Summary," *Institute for American Values,* September 9, 2003, http://www.americanvalues.org/html/hardwired_-_ex_summary.html (accessed March 29, 2012); C. B. Thomas and K. R. Duszynski, "Closeness to Parents and the Family Constellation in a Prospective Study of Five Disease States: Suicide, Mental Illness, Malignant Tumor, Hypertension, and Coronary Heart Disease," *Johns Hopkins Medical Journal,* 134, no. 5 (May 1974), 251-270.

2. St. Augustine, *Confessions* (New York: Penguin, 1961), 120.

3. Paraphrase of Blaisé Pascal, *Pensées* (New York: Penguin, 1997), 45.

4. Tim Keller, *Counterfeit Gods: The Empty Promises of Money, Sex and Power, and the Only Hope that Matters* (New York: Dutton/Penguin Group, 2009), xix–xx.

5. Gerald May, *Addiction and Grace: Love and Spirituality in the Healing of Addictions* (New York: HarperCollins, 1988), 3.

6. John Eldredge, *The Ransomed Heart: A Collection of Devotional Readings* (Nashville, Tennessee: Thomas Nelson, 2005), 223.

7. Mark Driscoll, "Worship and Idolatry," Sermon transcript available online at *Preach It, Teach It*, http://www.preachitteachit.org/uploads/tx_wecsermons/Mark_Driscoll_-_Worship_and_ Idolatry.pdf (accessed March 29, 2012).

8. Tim Keller, "The Two Lost Sons," 2009, Sermon transcript available online at Timothykeller .com, http://timothykeller.com/images/uploads/pdf/Sermon_Outline_3_The_Two_Lost_Sons .pdf (accessed March 29, 2012).

9. David Powlison, "Idols of the Heart and Vanity Fair," *The Journal of Biblical Counseling, 13*, no. 2 (Winter 1995): 34-50.

10. Keller, *Counterfeit Gods*, 155.

11. Philip Yancey, *Rumors of Another World* (Grand Rapids, Michigan: Zondervan, 2003), 145.

12. Jonathan Edwards, "The Christian Pilgrim," in *The Works of Jonathan Edwards*, ed. Edward Hickman, 2 vols. (1843; reprint, Edinburgh: Banner of Truth, 1974), 2:244.

Chapter 6: A New Affection

1. Henry Churchill King, *The Laws of Friendship, Human ad Divine* (New York: The MacMillan Company, 1919), 40.

2. Thomas Chalmers, "The Expulsive Power of a New Affection," *The Chautauquan, Volume 4* (Meadville, Pennsylvania: The Chautauqua Press, 1883), 388.

3. St. Augustine, *Sermons for Christians and Epiphany*, trans. Thomas Comerford Lawler, Ancient Christian Writers, no. 15 (Westminster, Maryland: Newman Press, 1953, 107.

4. Os Guinness, *The Call* (Nashville, Tennessee: Word Publishing, 1998), 4.

5. Eric Scalise, "Lifeline Lay Counselor Training Program," 2012.

Chapter 7: Reflections of Truth and Love

1. C. S. Lewis, *Prince Caspian* (New York: HarperCollins, 1951 and 1979), 218.

2. Thomas Merton, Ed. by Jonathan Montaldo, *A Year with Thomas Merton: Daily Meditations from His Journals* (New York: HarperCollins, 2004), 240.

3. John Bunyan as cited in John Brown, *John Bunyan: His Life, Times and Work* (New York: Houghton, Mifflin & Company, 1888), 175.

Chapter 8: Learning to Love Well

1. Tim Clinton and Gary Sibcy, *Why You Do the Things You Do* (Nashville, Tennessee: Thomas Nelson, 2006), 54.

2. Janae Weinhold and Barry Weinhold, *The Flight from Intimacy* (Novato, California: New World Library, 2008).

3. Robert Frost, "Mending Wall," *North of Boston* (New York: Henry Holt and Company, 1917).

4. Henry Cloud and John Townsend, Boundaries: *When to Say Yes, When to Say No, to Take Control of Your Life* (Grand Rapids, Michigan: Zondervan, 1992).

Chapter 9: Gaining a Secure Identity

1. Reggie Joiner and Carey Nieuwhof, *Parenting Beyond Your Capacity* (Colorado Springs, CO: David C. Cook, 2010). Page 27 states, "No one has more potential to influence your child than you."

2. Chart compiled from Tim Clinton and Gary Sibcy, *Loving Your Child Too Much* (Nashville, Tennessee: Thomas Nelson, 2006), 45-55.

3. Kenneth Adams, *Silently Seduced: When Parents Make their Children Partners—Understanding Covert Incest* (Deerfield Beach, Florida: Health Communications, Inc.,1991).

Chapter 11: Balancing Our Responsibilities

1. Lewis B. Smedes, *Forgive and Forget: Healing the Hurts We Don't Deserve* (New York: Harper-Collins, 1996), 144.

2. Reinhold Niebuhr as cited in Gordon Mursell, *The Story of Christian Spirituality: Two Thousand Years, from East to West* (Minneapolis, Minnesota: First Fortress Press, 2001), 354.

3. Henry Cloud and John Townsend, Boundaries: *When to Say Yes, When to Say No, to Take Control of Your Life* (Grand Rapids, Michigan: Zondervan, 1992), 29.

Chapter 13: Square Off Against Evil

1. Miroslav Volf, *Exclusion and Embrace: A Theological Exploration of Identity, Otherness, and Reconciliation*, (Nashville, Tennessee: Abingdon Press, 1996), 303-304.

2. C. S. Lewis, *Mere Christianity* (London: Geoffrey Bles, 1952), 91.

3. Philip Yancey, *What's So Amazing About Grace?* (Grand Rapids, Michigan: Zondervan, 2002).

4. Gary Inrig, *The Parables* (Grand Rapids, Michigan: Discovery House, 1991), 63.

5. Lewis B. Smedes, *The Art of Forgiving: When You Need To Forgive And Don't Know How*, (New York: Ballantine Books, 1996), 171.

6. Everett Worthington, *Handbook of Forgiveness* (New York: Routledge, 2005), 414.

7. Dan Allender, *The Healing Path* (Colorado Springs, Colorado: Water Brook Press, 1999), 5-6.

Chapter 14: When the Way Ahead is Difficult

1. Walter Ciszek, *He Leadeth Me* (Garden City, New York: Doubleday and Company, 1973), 38–182.

2. Timothy Gombis, *The Drama of Ephesians* (Downers Grove, Illinois: Intervarsity Press, 2010), 61-62.

3. Ibid., 76.

Chapter 15: The View from Tomorrow

1. Søren Kierkegaard as cited in Michael Strawser, *Both/And: Reading Kierkegaard from Irony to Edification* (New York: Fordham University Press, 1997), 17.

2. Alexander Solzhenitsyn, *The Gulag Archipelago* (New York: Random House, 2011).

3. C. S. Lewis, *The Horse and His Boy* (New York: HarperCollins, 1954 and 1982), 164.

Appendix: Break Through to Great Parenting

1. Stanley Greenspan, *The Challenging Child* (Cambridge, Massachusetts: Da Capo Press, 1995).

About the AACC

American Association of Christian Counselors

The American Association of Christian Counselors is an association of nearly 50,000 professional counselors, pastors, and lay leaders committed to biblical integrity and clinical excellence in Christian counseling and assisting members in the development of their own counseling practices.

The AACC exists to bring honor to Jesus Christ; to encourage and promote excellence in counseling worldwide; to disseminate information, educational resources, and counseling aids; to inspire the highest level of counselor training; and to contribute to the strengthening of families.

Membership is available to professional counselors, religious leaders, and lay counselors, as well as others who are interested in Christian counseling but who have little or no professional training. AACC members enjoy numerous benefits and receive several publications, including *Christian Counseling Today* magazine.

At the AACC, we understand the challenges in helping others. And whether you are a pastor, clinician, physician, or lay helper, we exist to serve you faithfully as you care for others. As a member, we'll help you become more aware of current trends and issues in counseling, deliver cutting-edge services and other timely resources—all designed to help increase your counseling effectiveness. As we grow together, we will work to:

1. Help you use the Bible with confidence when dealing with life's most difficult and trying issues.
2. Offer insight on counseling issues and patterns that have emerged through reflection, research, and scholarship.
3. Provide practical tools and strategies to help you in your day-to-day ministry.
4. Offer standards and direction in handling the tough legal, ethical, and gray areas of counseling.

For more information, visit www.aacc.net or call 1-800-526-8673.

Dr. Tim Clinton, LPC, LMFT, is president of the nearly 50,000-member American Association of Christian Counselors (AACC) and founder of Light University Online, which has over 160,000 students enrolled. He is also the professor of counseling and executive director of the Center for Counseling and Family Studies at Liberty University.

Pat Springle is the founder of Baxter Press and coauthor of the classic work, *Codependency*. Pat served on the staff of Campus Crusade for Christ and was an executive with Rapha Treatment Centers. Springle has authored or coauthored more than fifty books.

WORTHY
P U B L I S H I N G

IF YOU LIKED THIS BOOK...

- Tell your friends by going to: www.break-through-book .com and clicking "LIKE"
- Share the video book trailer by posting it on your Facebook page
- Head over to facebook.com/worthypublishing, click "LIKE" and post a comment regarding what you enjoyed about the book
- Tweet "I recommend reading #BreakThroughBook by @ DrTimClinton @Worthypub"
- Hashtag: #BreakThrough
- Subscribe to our newsletter by going to www.worthy publishing.com

WORTHY PUBLISHING
FACEBOOK PAGE

WORTHY PUBLISHING
WEBSITE